Praise for

SAY YES TO GOD

Say Yes to God should come with a warning label — like "flammable" or "explosive." Books this raw and real don't come along often, especially from highly visible leaders with global impact. Read it at your own risk — but take the risk!

BILL HYBELS, author of *The Power of a Whisper*

○

Kay Warren, like it says in Robert Frost's famous poem, "took the road less traveled by, and that has made all the difference."

RICH STEARNS, president of World Vision U.S.

○

Kay Warren is touching the conscience of a nation.

JOHN ORTBERG, author of *The Life You've Always Wanted*

○

Kay Warren's story of surrender to a deeper meaning demonstrates the way to make sense of the chaos and jubilation that characterize our existence. Through Kay's human and humble submission, we learn, as Kay did when she decided to form the "Seriously Disturbed and Gloriously Ruined Club," that we cannot afford to remain indifferent.

Her Excellency, JEANNETTE KAGAME, First Lady of Rwanda

Kay's intimate portrait of brokenness reminds us of what surrender to God ultimately produces — a person with God's own heart for the hurting. It is a deeply moving story that a watching, suffering world needs to see in the church today.

WESS STAFFORD, president of Compassion International

○

Kay's book is an unmistakable sign of a new evangelicalism that is closer to the poor — and anything but safe!

SHANE CLAIBORNE, author of *The Irresistible Revolution*

○

Kay's book forced me to clarify my calling and grapple with how much I'm willing to pay to follow it faithfully. I needed to read this.

LYNNE HYBELS, author of *Nice Girls Don't Change the World*

○

Kay Warren suffers from a case of severe compassion. That's why I admire her. Only read this book if you want a softer heart.

MAX LUCADO, author of *Facing the Giants*

○

Say Yes to God will inspire you, challenge you, humble you, make you uncomfortable, and show how God can use you to make a difference in the world.

DENNIS RAINEY, author of *Growing a Spiritually Strong Family*

This beautiful book is an astonishing achievement, the words of a modern-day prophet. Many chapters are stand-alone classics. It is one of the richest reads I have experienced. It breathes the spirit of Jesus on every page — so powerful, so well written, and so profound.

GARY THOMAS, author of *Authentic Faith*

o

Be careful. While reading this book, you may wrestle with an angel as Jacob did, and limp with joy in the continuing discovery of surrender and privilege in serving Jesus.

DEBORAH DORTZBACH, international director
for HIV/AIDS programs, World Relief

o

Kay Warren is an unflagging lioness. More than simply a call to an awakening to global suffering, this book is a primer in Christlike obedience that anyone can consider.

STEVE HAAS, vice president of World Vision U.S.

o

Say Yes to God is a wake-up call for the church. No ministry can afford to avoid her trip through the AIDS crisis. Kay not only tells her story but gives readers real resources to bring the fight against HIV home.

DAVID MILLER, board member of The AIDS
Institute

In this challenging work by my friend Kay Warren, you will experience the adventure of surrendering fully to the purposes of God for your life. After reading *Say Yes to God*, you will never be the same.

DR. LOIS EVANS, senior vice president of
The Urban Alternative

O

If you think this is a book about how to be the wife of a successful minister, you're wrong. It's the story of someone who models the journey from self-interest religiosity to unconditionally loving Christ by embracing the lepers of our own age — the victims of HIV/AIDS.

TONY CAMPOLO, professor emeritus,
Eastern University

O

Kay's *Say Yes to God* is a bell toll for us all. If we trust in God with all our hearts, his divine will for healing and health will unfold one person at a time. All we need to do is surrender and say yes to God.

DR. ROBERT REDFIELD, director, division of clinical
care and research, Institute of Human Virology

KAY WARREN

SAY YES TO GOD

A CALL TO COURAGEOUS SURRENDER

FORMERLY *DANGEROUS SURRENDER*, NOW UPDATED AND EXPANDED

ZONDERVAN®

ZONDERVAN.com/
AUTHOR**TRACKER**
follow your favorite authors

ZONDERVAN

Say Yes to God
Copyright © 2010 by Kay Warren

Formerly *Dangerous Surrender*
Copyright © 2007 by Kay Warren

This title is also available as a Zondervan ebook. Visit www.zondervan.com/ebooks.

This title is also available in a Zondervan audio edition. Visit www.zondervan.fm.

Requests for information should be addressed to:

Zondervan, *Grand Rapids, Michigan 49530*

Library of Congress Cataloging-in-Publication Data

Warren, Kay, 1954–
      Say yes to God : a call to courageous surrender / Kay Warren.
            p.   cm.
      Rev. ed. of: Dangerous surrender.
      Includes bibliographical references.
      ISBN 978-0-310-32836-0 (softcover)
      1. Submissiveness—Religious aspects—Christianity. 2. Providence and
government of God. 3. Service (Theology). 4. Spirituality. I. Warren, Kay, 1954–
Dangerous surrender. II. Title.
      BV4647.A25W37   2007
      248.4—dc22   2010026283

All Scripture quotations, unless otherwise indicated, are taken from the Holy Bible, *New International Version®, NIV®.* Copyright © 1973, 1978, 1984 by Biblica, Inc.™ Used by permission of Zondervan. All rights reserved worldwide.

Other Bible translations quoted in this book are listed on pages 249–50, which hereby become a part of this copyright page.

Any Internet addresses (websites, blogs, etc.) and telephone numbers printed in this book are offered as a resource. They are not intended in any way to be or imply an endorsement by Zondervan, nor does Zondervan vouch for the content of these sites and numbers for the life of this book.

Cover design: Faceout Studio
Cover photography: Shutterstock®
Interior design: Beth Shagene

Printed in the United States of America

10 11 12 13 14 15 /DCI/ 21 20 19 18 17 16 15 14 13 12 11 10 9 8 7 6 5 4 3 2 1

To the HIV-positive people I've met
over the past eight years.
You have enriched my life!
I've been broken by your suffering
and inspired by your courage.
I join you in praying
for the day when AIDS will end.

My King, the Lord Jesus Christ,
I owe it all to you.
I am your bond servant;
do with me as you please.
My love for you is beyond words,
and my gratitude can only be measured
by my life offered in your service.
My answer will always be yes.

CONTENTS

1. The Leap of Faith   11

2. The Kingdom of Me   41

3. Gloriously Ruined   69

4. Ready, Set, Stop   87

5. Exposing Evil   107

6. Mirrors Don't Lie   133

7. The Gift of Presence   149

8. A Deliberate Choice   165

9. An Unexpected Bond   181

10. Linking Arms   199

11. What Are You Willing to Die For?   217

The Adventure Continues   237

Resources   243

Acknowledgments   245

Bible Translations   249

Notes   251

Readers' Group Discussion Guide   253

About Kay Warren   269

THE LEAP OF FAITH

*"Much is required from those
to whom much is given."*
Luke 12:48 LB

*If through a broken heart God can bring
His purposes to pass in the world,
then thank Him for breaking your heart.*
Oswald Chambers, *My Utmost for His Highest*, November 1

I DIDN'T SEE IT COMING.

I woke up on a normal day, looking ahead to a typical schedule. Nothing out of the ordinary was planned — routine stuff filled the calendar slots. I didn't have the faintest clue that God was about to rock my world and change the trajectory of my life forever.

Unaware of the radical change in store for me on that spring day in 2002, I sat down on the couch in my living room with a cup of tea and picked up one of the weekly newsmagazines we subscribe to. I noticed that there was a story about AIDS in Africa, and I casually flipped over to that section, not because I cared about AIDS in Africa (I didn't care about AIDS anywhere, let alone in Africa), but because I wanted to stay up on current events. As I began to read, I quickly realized that the graphic pictures that accompanied the article were horrific — skeletal men and women, children so weak they couldn't brush the flies from their faces. I couldn't look at them. But for some strange reason, I was compelled to continue reading. I partially covered my eyes with my hands and tried to peek through the cracks in my fingers at the words without looking at the faces of dying men, women, and children.

God, in his wisdom, knew exactly how to bypass my feeble attempts to block out the upsetting photographs. If he couldn't get my attention with the pictures, he would use the words. The phrase "twelve million children orphaned due to AIDS in Africa" jumped off the magazine page and imprinted itself in my mind. I was shocked and stunned and, frankly, disbelieving. "No," I said out loud, "there's no way there could be twelve million children orphaned in one place due to one illness at one time. I don't even know one orphan — how could there be twelve million?" I threw the magazine on the floor in horror.

But I couldn't get rid of this new reality so easily. That night, I was haunted by the thought of twelve million boys and girls left alone, their parents the victims of AIDS. As I drifted into sleep, my last thought was about the orphans; I woke up in the morning with their little faces swirling through my mind. Suddenly AIDS, Africa, and orphans were everywhere! Every newspaper I picked up had an article about AIDS in Africa; it seemed as though every newscast echoed the story. Over the next few weeks, I tried to escape the stories and the pictures, but I couldn't.

God and I began an intense internal conversation. At the time, I thought our conversation was about AIDS. In retrospect, I understand that we were beginning a discussion about something even bigger. *Surrender.* Surrender to the God of the universe. But God knew I wasn't ready to see that surrender was the real subject. After all, I already considered myself fully surrendered to Jesus Christ. No need to discuss that any further, right? But AIDS, that was something I knew God and I had to talk about.

My first argument with him was over the numbers of people infected by HIV — the virus that causes AIDS — and the number of orphans left in its wake. I reasoned to myself that the media must be exaggerating the numbers. Since I considered myself pretty savvy about global situations, surely I would *know* if a problem of this magnitude existed.

As the days went by, the internal dialogue with God continued unabated, but it also began to shift focus. I gradually began to accept that while I had been raising my family and serving in my church, a humanitarian crisis of gargantuan proportions had been escalating on our planet. There was no media exaggeration, no propaganda to garner sympathy for a minor cause. Something tragic and terrible was happening right under my nose.

I felt powerless to do anything about the new reality thrust in front of me. I cried out to God, "Why are you bothering me with this? There's nothing I can do about it. I'm just an ordinary person. What could one person do about such a gigantic problem? And by the way, in case you haven't noticed, I'm a white suburban mom with a minivan. What do I know about a disease in Africa?"

After a month of anguished wrestling with God, I reached a point at which I had to make a conscious decision. Would I retreat to my comfortable life and my settled plans, pretending

I didn't know about the HIV/AIDS pandemic and the millions of orphans? Or would I surrender to God's call — now so obvious I could not deny it — and let my heart engage with a cause I was pretty sure would include buckets of pain and sorrow? I didn't know what would happen if I said yes to God's increasingly strong urge to engage. What did *engaging* even mean? I felt like I was standing on the edge of a giant precipice. I couldn't go back, and yet the way forward looked like stepping into a void. God was calling me to surrender to his call on my life, even if I didn't yet understand what he expected me to do.

The moment of decision had arrived. With eyes closed and teeth clenched tightly, I finally said yes. The second I did, my heart broke, and I was *shattered*. It was as though God took my heart and put it through a wood chipper — what went in was a "branch" but what came out on the other side was a heart shredded into a million pieces. With lightning speed, God yanked the blindfold of apathy, ignorance, and complacency from my eyes, and I was overcome by the realities of the suffering he revealed. I ached with a new kind of pain — a pain that felt as though it had come from the most visceral part of me. I was filled with sorrow and grief. I wept as though I was the one who was sick, or my child was dying, or I was the orphan left alone. I knew next to nothing about HIV/AIDS, but my heart was instantly linked with those who know it intimately. Like the apostle Paul knocked off his donkey on the road to Damascus (see Acts 9), I was changed by my encounter with truth.

I became a seriously disturbed woman.

Suddenly I became consumed with a desire to learn about HIV/AIDS. I devoured every book, article, and video I could get my hands on. I searched the Internet for websites that could teach me about this global crisis. I consulted health care professionals. I put out feelers through all of my contacts, searching for anyone who could help me understand how HIV/AIDS began, what was known about it, and what could be done. I was disturbed — almost frantic — in my hurry to make up for lost time.

DISTURBED

The word *disturbed* is often associated with mental illness and instability. We say, "He's disturbed," when we describe someone who reacts in an overly emotional way or appears troubled emotionally. I want to redefine this word, because I believe that God is looking for some disturbed people. He is searching for men and women, students, and young adults who will allow him to disturb them by making them truly see the world in which we live — so disturbed that they will be compelled to do something about what they see.

Most of us have grown up in a culture that promotes precisely the opposite approach. Parents tell their children, "Never talk about politics or religion; it makes people uncomfortable." And for the most part, we've obeyed this cultural edict. Instead of tackling uncomfortable topics, we talk about the latest TV reality show or the hot sports figures or the price of gasoline. Believers are just as guilty as nonbelievers! Even worse, we refuse to talk about the painful, disturbing subjects — child prostitution, child labor, rape, poverty, injustice, ethnic hatred, greed, materialism, environmental destruction, HIV/AIDS. These are disturbing topics. But if we're not disturbed by the world in which we live, we will be consumed with the trivial, the insignificant, and the temporary. We will spend our days pursuing all the wrong goals, living by the wrong measurements of success, evaluating our legacy by the wrong standards.

Jesus' words "Much is required from those to whom much is given" (Luke 12:48 LB) began to reverberate inside my mind, taking their place alongside the disturbing images I had seen. I had been given so much — what was my responsibility in return? God clearly tells us that we are "to act justly and to love mercy and to walk humbly with [our] God" (Micah 6:8). I began to wonder how to apply this truth to my life. How does becoming a seriously disturbed person affect the way I live?

I soon realized that the first area of my life to be shaken up would be my approach to personal comfort. Instead of being disturbed, I was comfortable. I had no complaints. My material needs were more than met. I lived in a beautiful part of the country. I enjoyed a rich and satisfying marriage. My children made me proud. I had meaningful friendships that provided companionship and fun. I was involved at my church in multiple ministries that I loved.

It's very easy for us to remain aloof and untouched by the suffering that defines the existence of the vast majority of people on this planet. I have read that if you have food in your refrigerator, clothes on your back, a roof overhead, and a place to sleep, you are richer than 75 percent of the people in this world! If you have *any* money in the bank and some in your wallet and some spare change in a dish somewhere, you are among the top 8 percent of the world's wealthy; 92 percent have less to live on than you do! If you have never experienced the danger of battle, the loneliness of imprisonment, the agony of torture, or the pangs of starvation, you are ahead of 500 million other people in the world. If you can attend worship services at church without the fear of harassment, arrest, torture, or death, you are more blessed than three billion people in the world.

I don't tell you this to make you feel guilty — but I do hope you feel uncomfortable. I hope these statistics disturb you. God in his sovereignty decided where you would be born and allowed you to live in a place that has almost everything anyone could ever desire, so there is no guilt that he has ordered our lives in such a way. The only guilt we bear is the guilt of ignoring the men, women, and children of this world who do not have what we have — the guilt of spending the majority of our time, money, and resources exclusively on ourselves and our families. *That* is legitimate guilt.

Let's just say that something is beginning to stir in your soul as you read. What should you do about it? Where should you begin? What is God's will for you and for the broken world you inhabit?

One thing I know for sure: God's will begins with surrender.

COURAGEOUS SURRENDER

Someone once asked me to define Christianity in one word, and after some reflection, I responded, "Surrender. It all boils down to surrender." Everything I know about a personal relationship with Jesus Christ begins and ends with surrender — with saying yes to God. That tiny one-syllabic word initiates an exhilarating, life-altering adventure.

So why is *surrender* a dirty word to many of us with

mostly negative connotations? Some synonyms are *give in, give up, admit defeat, lay down your arms, submit, yield, capitulate.* Surrender implies failure, a decision made only when irrevocably backed into a corner, a concession by the conquered to the conquerors, a tattered white flag waving weakly. No wonder we avoid talking about surrender. It's not very attractive to those who see themselves as strong. One of the most deeply held illusions by those of us in the West is that we are tough and independent and quite sure we don't need anyone else. We carry these illusions into our spiritual lives as well, and doing so keeps many from following Christ. "Surrender to God? No thanks. I can do life by myself." Even those of us who have acknowledged our need for Jesus Christ to be our Savior have a difficult time surrendering our will to him on a daily basis; we're just too full of ourselves, too much in control, too proud.

From God's perspective, however, "I surrender" are the most beautiful words he ever hears us speak. To him, our saying yes to his will has only positive connotations. Surrendering means that we have come to the end of our independence from him, our reliance on self-sufficiency, and our insistence that we don't need him. Surrender to God changes everything!

I'll explore this concept further in the next chapter, but here at the start, please know that surrendering your life to God is the boldest and riskiest step you can take. Being courageously surrendered to God allows you to know him in increasingly deeper ways and to participate fully in his will.

THE DEVELOPING PHOTOGRAPH

Before that spring day in 2002, I thought I knew what God's will was for that stage of my life. Rick and I were entering the empty-nest season. Our youngest son was a senior in high school, and we had our lives planned out. We share a deep love for pastors and missionaries and thoroughly enjoy using our spiritual gifts of teaching. We anticipated that the second half of our lives would be spent traveling the world, teaching and encouraging ministry couples. It was a really good plan for our future.

It just wasn't God's plan.

Through the years, I've found that discovering God's will often resembles looking at an undeveloped Polaroid photograph. When the camera spits out the picture, the images are gray and shapeless, but the longer you look at the picture the clearer it becomes. The day I said yes to caring about people with HIV/AIDS, God handed me a fuzzy Polaroid picture. I didn't know exactly what he wanted me to do. I had no agenda, no plan in mind, no long-range strategy — I just knew I couldn't face God someday and tell him I had ignored the suffering of millions of people just because it made me uncomfortable or because I didn't know what to do about it. The picture didn't grow sharp and clear instantaneously, but over the course of several years, it has become increasingly clear. I now "see" more of what God has in mind for my role in stopping the AIDS pandemic.

Of course, with the advent of digital technology, Polaroid cameras are becoming outdated. Now we're impatient with such a slow process — we want instant clarity! We don't want to wait for the picture to develop. When we sense God's leading us on a new journey, we want all of the information up front. We want God to fill out the travel forms in triplicate, give us a detailed road map before we start the journey, and guarantee our safe arrival at the destination. We want the rewards of living lives of faith without actually having to demonstrate faith. For you to become a seriously disturbed, surrendered person of faith, you will have to be willing to say yes in advance — to give God your answer before you've heard the question.

My friend Gary Thomas frequently challenges me to grow spiritually through his insights that probe beneath the surface of my faith. He writes, "I learned that faith isn't tested by how often God answers my prayers with a yes but by my willingness to continue serving him and thanking him, even when I don't have a clue as to what he is doing."[1]

We tend to think that only the superstars — the brilliant high achievers, those with head-turning good looks, the naturally gifted athletes — can make a difference in the world through their courageous surrender. The great news is that God's plan for getting his work done in the world includes more than superstars. Ordinary men and women can be part of a miracle by saying yes to God.

"Now all glory to God, who is able, through his mighty power at work within us, to accomplish infinitely more than we might ask or think" (Ephesians 3:20 NLT).

ORDINARY

I look back on the day God captured my attention and turned it toward people living with HIV/AIDS and realize that I didn't see it coming for a number of reasons, but mostly because it never occurred to me that I had anything significant to offer to a global problem. I have never seen myself as a particularly gifted or talented person — just as someone average and quite ordinary.

When I was little, I wanted to be a great student in school, but my best efforts never landed me on the dean's list or qualified me for academic scholarships. I was just average. Because I was a pastor's daughter, everyone expected I would learn how to play the piano, so I took lessons. I had visions of myself on a grand tour, playing magnificently for appreciative audiences, perhaps even recording an album or two of my music. I discovered that while I can play the piano, I'm just average. No one will ever ask me to produce a CD of classical music, and no tours have ever been lined up. I realized I was average academically and in the talent department, but I held out hope for a while that I would turn into a gorgeous Miss America type. In fact, I used to wait eagerly for the annual pageant. I longed to have the perfect body and face that all Miss America contestants possess. I studied my bathroom mirror for signs of a budding beauty, but none came. While no one has told me I'm ugly, I've never walked into a room and heard audible gasps from those present who are stunned by my beauty! I'm just average.

By the time Rick and I had married, I was pretty discouraged by the way my life was turning out. I was so average, so *nothing*. You'd think I would have married some average Joe to go along with my own perceived average status, but instead I married a superstar. Rick was always at the top of everything he put his hand to — always! He did great in school. He was popular, talented, and self-confident. He was the president of every club he ever joined, and the trophy case in his living room was crowded with the awards he and his younger sister, Chaundel, had accumulated. He had big dreams for his life. But one summer while working as a lifeguard at a Christian camp, Rick committed his life to Christ, and a new dream was born. His focus changed from business to ministry, and he became a passionate follower of Jesus Christ.

After Rick graduated from seminary in Fort Worth, Texas, we moved back to our native California and started the Saddleback Valley Community Church in 1980. With Rick at the helm, the church grew exponentially — both in numbers and in spiritual depth. I was still a fish out of water, struggling to figure out where I fit. He was a superstar; I was more like a "twinkle little star." A couple of years into the planting of the church, however, God and I had an encounter that became a linchpin moment — one I could look back to over and over again to draw strength from.

I had been asked to be the speaker at one of our women's events, and I reluctantly agreed. I was working with the children of our church at that time because kids were safe — I didn't worry that they would judge me to be inadequate; I figured they didn't care if I told the Bible story backward or sideways. On the way to the event, I began to cry and have a pity party — something I did on a regular basis: "God, you have made the most dreadful mistake. Why didn't you make me better? You should have given Rick a different wife — someone prettier, more talented, more gifted, more intelligent. I just can't measure up." I don't cry in an attractive way — with just a few tears my eyes get red and swollen shut — so I turned on the radio to try to distract myself from my angst.

Then it happened!

Playing on the radio at that exact moment was a song sent from God's heart to mine:

Ordinary People

Just ordinary people,
God uses ordinary people.
He chooses people just like me and you
Who are willing to do as He commands.
God uses people that will give Him all,
No matter how small your all may seem to you;
Because little becomes much as you place it in the
  Master's hand.
Oh, just like that little lad
Who gave Jesus all he had;
How the multitude was fed
With the fish and the loaves of bread.
What you have may not seem much,
But when you yield it to the touch
Of the Master's loving hand, yes,
Then you'll understand how your life could never be
  *the same.**

Danniebelle Hall

Now the tears really flowed, but instead of self-pitying tears, they were tears of joy and peace. God chose *me* to be an ordinary person! He could have made me smarter, more talented, and more beautiful if he had chosen to — but his hands lovingly shaped me just the way he wanted me to be. Why? Because my ordinariness, when surrendered to God,

---

* Lyrics by Danniebelle Hall, Forever Danniebelle Ministries. Used by permission of EMI Christian Music Group. All rights reserved.

allows him to make a miracle out of my life in much the same way as when he fed thousands of hungry people with two tiny fish and five loaves of bread nearly two thousand years ago. Truly, little becomes much when we place it in his hands.

That day, I offered all that I am and all that I am not to him. I said, "God, I'm so sick of whining and complaining that I'm just average. Forgive me for accusing you of making a mistake when you made me. From now on, I accept with joy your decision to make me average. I *surrender* myself to you. Use me whenever, wherever, and in whatever way you choose. God, I don't have much to offer to you. My "lunch" seems to be just a baloney sandwich — will you miraculously multiply it?" That simple but honest prayer of surrender was the most dangerous decision I had ever made.

In Matthew 9:28 – 30 (NLT), Jesus asked some folks, " 'Do you believe I can make you see?' 'Yes, Lord,' they told him, 'we do.' Then he touched their eyes and said, 'Because of your faith, it will happen.' Then their eyes were opened, and they could see!"

So it's not the magnitude or magnificence of the spiritual gifts we offer back to God that opens the door to miracles, but the simple faith that takes him up on his promise to do more than we could ever ask or think. This means that miracles are within your reach too, no matter how ordinary you consider yourself to be.

The last twenty-five years have provided countless opportunities for me to live up to my promise to be happy with who I am and who God has made me to be. He received the surrender of my ordinariness and has multiplied my meager offerings again and again. I have spent many years developing the gift of teaching I discovered when I stopped being afraid of all of the comparisons to Rick. I was totally satisfied with my plans for future speaking and teaching around the world. But God interrupted my plans and seriously disturbed me on that fateful day when I read a magazine article about HIV/AIDS in Africa.

MODELS OF SURRENDER

In this journey of becoming more fully surrendered to God, I've benefited greatly from role models — other people who show me the way to becoming yielded to God. Jesus' mother, Mary, has been a model of surrender for me. In fact, more than any other character in Scripture, Mary embodies the full extent of what it means to surrender oneself to God. She was a flesh-and-blood woman who made an astonishing commitment to put herself at God's disposal when the angel announced to her that she would carry the Savior in her womb. The rest of her life offered her the opportunity to make good on that promise. Would she *really* trust God? Would she trust him enough to say yes without knowing where her surrender would take her?

There was nothing about Mary from an outward perspective that would make her worthy of "Who's Who in Israel" or any list of "Most Widely Admired Women," let alone qualify her to carry the Son of God in her body. She was young, poor, and probably uneducated — yet God honored her with a responsibility that most of us would run from. She could have argued long and hard with the angel who announced God's selection of her to give birth to God's Son, pointing out the obvious reasons he was making a big mistake. She

SAY YES TO GOD

could have made reasonable excuses for declining this "generous offer," perhaps even suggesting a few of her girlfriends whom God might consider instead. As unthinkable as it is from our vantage point in history, she could have flat-out refused. But her feeble protests quickly died. Having no idea what her yes would mean for her, she surrendered: "Behold the handmaid of the Lord; be it unto me according to thy word" (Luke 1:38 KJV). *That* is courageous surrender!

Mary yielded her body to become the place where the Savior developed and grew. She abandoned her previously stellar reputation to the village gossips, who gleefully speculated about her private life. She opened her heart wide to love a child as only a mother can. She watched him become a man who baffled her, confused her, and most likely even wounded her by his refusal to take Joseph's place in the carpenter shop. She followed him around during the three years of his public ministry, probably hoping just to be near him. With growing dread, she watched his popularity wane as he failed to live up to her people's erroneous idea of what the Messiah would look like. Finally, she learned the news that he had been arrested, beaten beyond recognition, and offered as a substitute for a convicted criminal named Barabbas.

A lifetime of saying yes culminated in that awful day when she stood near his cross, shattered by the sight of this precious child of hers hated, bleeding, broken, hanging from a tree — and still she said yes. There is no record of her lashing out at God in her grief, accusing him of giving her a raw deal, of misleading her into this place of extreme agony. There is no rescinding of her yes. Even her broken heart was given back to the One who had chosen her to be used for his purposes. She saw her son viciously slaughtered, placed in a tomb, resurrected, and then gone forever — this time back to heaven. Would saying yes *ever* bring joy to Mary's soul — or would her yes always come with a knife to the heart?

Later, in the book of Acts, we're told that Mary was with the 120 disciples who were hiding in the upper room after Jesus ascended to heaven, and she was probably there when the Holy Spirit was given to all believers. Finally there is release, redemption, answers to her questions. Surrendered faith makes sense; the picture is finally clear. But Mary didn't wait until all was crystal clear to surrender herself to God. She didn't insist that God's will come with no suffering attached. She simply said, "I am the Lord's servant. May everything you have said about me come true" (Luke 1:38 NLT).

I can imagine you may be tempted to brush past Mary because her story happened so long ago; and let's face it — there will never be another person who is asked to be the mother of God! It's easy to disconnect from her surrender because it feels so far removed from the world we live in. But it's not so easy to ignore the stories of ordinary men and women still living today. Throughout these chapters, I'll introduce you to people I've met who have encountered God and been challenged to surrender their lives to him. It all starts with a willingness to place no limits on what God can do in our lives. We cannot dictate to him what we will or will not allow.

Another significant role model for me in learning how to surrender completely to God is François Fénelon. He was a highly respected French priest who was appointed by King Louis XIV to tutor his grandson and future heir to the throne. His writings never fail to make me examine the depth of my commitment to Christ. Consider this:

To want to serve God in some conditions, but not others, is to serve Him in your own way. But to put no limits on your submission to God is truly dying to yourself. This is how to worship God. Open yourself to God without measure. Let His life flow through you like a torrent. Fear nothing on the road you are walking. God will lead you by the hand. Let your love for Him cast out the fear you feel for yourself.[2]

Dave and Carolyn McClendon's life had slowed down. Their children were grown. Dave had retired from Coca Cola, and Carolyn from Boeing. Then they heard a message I delivered about HIV/AIDS and God's compassion for the sick. They were intrigued and came to a training session we hosted for those interested in volunteering at a local AIDS clinic in their neighborhood. They responded by saying, "Yes, whatever we can do, Lord." What began as spending a few hours a week driving HIV-positive clients to their doctors turned into helping at the food pantry, which led to recruiting friends, neighbors, and small group members to volunteer. Month after month, they found their lives increasingly intertwined with the men and women who were seeking care at the clinic, and before long, they met a very sick Cambodian woman with a young daughter, whom Dave and Carolyn befriended. To their surprise, the mother asked Dave and Carolyn if they would become her daughter's guardians if she died. What could Dave and Carolyn say? How could they possibly turn down this tender request? How could they look into the mother's eyes and tell her they would not care for her treasured little girl? They said yes.

Dave and Carolyn are now co-guardians of an eleven-year-old girl. She spends five or more days and nights a week at their home. The McClendons' guardianship involves a variety of responsibilities and privileges that range from helping with homework to teaching her how to ride a bike, from taking her on fun outings to the zoo and Disneyland to taking her to church and teaching her about God's love — right down to tending to the mundane details of doctor visits. The mother and daughter have been enveloped into Dave and Carolyn's entire family, where they participate in all family dinners and celebrations. Dave and Carolyn told God that they would do whatever he wanted them to do, that they wouldn't put any limits on what he could do with them in their surrender — and God took them seriously.

How does reading the McClendons' story make you feel? Inspired, or maybe uneasy? If their story (or anything else you've read so far) has made you nervous, you may be tempted to read the rest of this book "peeking through the cracks" in your fingers — afraid to read it yet afraid to put it down. I'm tempted to try to relieve any discomfort you might be feeling and tell you it will all be OK — that the road chosen for you won't have many bumps or potholes, that Mary was an anomaly and most people don't suffer the way she did, that very soon the billions of people who are suffering in our world today will have enough to eat, effective medicine for their sicknesses, and clean water to drink. I'd like to say that this first chapter is the hardest one and that it will only get easier from here on out.

But I can't.

God is longing to *seriously disturb* you about his world. He's searching for men and women, students, young people and old people, people of every race and from every tribe, who will recklessly abandon themselves to him and surrender to his purposes. The Polaroid picture may not be sharp and clear at this moment, and you may be wondering, "What will courageous surrender look like for me?" On the other hand, you may have a solid plan for your life already laid out, as Rick and I did. The question for you, then, is this: Is it God's plan? Either way, your decision at this moment is about saying yes to God—like Jesus' mother, Mary; like Dave and Carolyn; like me—regardless of whether you can see where that yes will take you. My challenge to you is that you would say, "I don't know exactly what the question is, God, but my answer is yes!"

I need to make you aware of something as we get started on this journey together. If you choose to say yes to God, your life will become radically different. When Jesus sent out the twelve in his name, their message was startling: "They preached with joyful urgency that life can be radically different" (Mark 6:12 MSG).

I imagine there are at least two distinct reactions to the idea that life can be radically different. You may instantly panic—"I don't want life to be radically different! It's fine the way it is. It's predictable, stable, secure. It's running smoothly at the moment. Why in the world would I want to shake it up?" For those who are comfortable, life is good enough.

Or you may panic for a very different reason. Your life is in chaos, and you're terrified of rocking the boat even further. You might wonder, "What will happen if I make changes? Will my spouse or loved ones still accept me? Will I be rejected or ridiculed for being a Jesus freak? What will it cost me to say yes to God?"

Perhaps you will not panic but respond with praise. You

are desperate for a radical change. Your life isn't working anymore, and everything is out of whack. You're open to just about any suggestion that comes down the pike. You are searching for relief from the pain, the brokenness, and the constant sense of failure and guilt. Or perhaps life is not as much painful as it is stale, boring, and utterly predictable. The hope that your life could be radically different causes you to shout, "Praise God!" This news is like a life preserver thrown to a drowning person.

Regardless of where you fit on the scale of panic to praise, or whether or not you believe it yet, the Bible clearly asserts that life *can* be radically different. The disciples were insistent in their message — they spoke with "joyful urgency." So I, too, speak to you in this moment with joyful urgency: Life can be radically different! It starts by saying yes to God.

Two things I know for sure. When you respond to God, your days will become an adventure, and you will see miracles.

Paul, in 1 Corinthians 1:9 (MSG), writes, "God, who got you started in this spiritual adventure, shares with us the life of his Son and our Master Jesus." God tells us we are not only on a spiritual journey; we are on a spiritual adventure as well. We are hot-wired for adventure.

Most of us thrill to the stories of people who decide to sell all their belongings and sail around the world, stopping in exotic places on every continent, deaf to the threats of hurricanes, rogue waves, or pirates. We are fascinated when someone lays it all on the line by venturing on a solo flight around the world, betting that their navigational devices will perform perfectly, weather will cooperate, and lightning won't strike. We are riveted by those who skate on thin ice by climbing Mount Everest and K2, ignoring the perils of avalanche, oxygen deprivation, and whiteouts. I am still incredulous when I hear that NASA has launched another spaceship into orbit. I don't get it! Why do people willingly strap themselves into a tiny capsule behind gigantic rockets and allow themselves to be violently thrust into outer space? I watch the takeoffs and landings as though I'm watching a futuristic sci-fi movie, not quite convinced that this is real.

Many of us voraciously read stories and watch movies about mythological heroes from the past — great warriors who conquered lands and vanquished kingdoms. They slew the fearsome dragons and rescued gorgeous damsels in distress. There is something deep inside of us that resonates with these tales of adventure, quest, and exploits.

A hundred years ago, Sir Ernest Shackleton was looking for men who would accompany him on an expedition to the South Pole. He put this ad in London newspapers: "Men wanted for hazardous journey. Small wages, bitter cold, long months of complete darkness, constant danger, safe return doubtful. Honor and recognition in case of success."[3]

The fact is, God has an adventure for all of us! We instinctively know it, and we yearn for it. When we say yes to God, he will take us places, both externally into the world and internally on a journey with him, unlike any we've ever been to before.

Look at what happened to Abraham when he said yes to God. "By an act of faith, Abraham said yes to God's call to travel to an unknown place that would become his home. When he left he had no idea where he was going" (Hebrews 11:8 MSG).

Abraham takes his place alongside the mythical heroes

who conquered mountains, countries, seas, and space. He was a flesh-and-blood man who was willing to risk it all, uproot his family, and follow God into an unknown future.

Unfortunately, most of us have settled for something a lot less than a life of adventure. Our dreams of adventure, exploits, and quests have shrunk to the size of watching reality TV. We laugh at the truly stupid folks on *Jackass* who put themselves in jeopardy for a chance at fifteen minutes of fame. Or we get excited over the smallest sense of personal accomplishment — like conquering our fear of riding a roller coaster.

Admit it — some of you have stood in line for rides like Viper and Screamer, anxiously biting your fingernails, your stomach in a knot, wondering if you can do it. Then as you exit the ride, you high-five your buddy, screaming "Yeah!" as though what you just did really counted as courage.

Many of us have reduced our inner thirst for adventure to an even smaller level. The lands you conquer and the dragons you slay are in cyberspace. In *Warcraft* — or any of the dozens of other online games — you're part of either the Horde or the Alliance. Your character performs amazing feats of bold battle, and you live for the hours of free time every day when you enter a universe you can control. You are an adventurer!

Maybe the biggest dragon you slay is fighting your way through traffic every morning on the way to work. "Damsels in distress" usually refers to women like me who are attempting to juggle work and home demands; doing their best to coordinate their kids' schedules — dance lessons, soccer practice, swim lessons, and homework in between meals on the run and unfinished projects.

Our existence has shrunk to this very tiny world. Is this the best we can do? Is this all we can hope for? Thank God, the answer is no. God has an *adventure* for our days!

It is completely ironic that I am joyfully urging you to seek adventure, to take risks, to make decisions with courageous surrender. I have always been the biggest chicken, the wimpiest of wimps, the scarediest of scaredy-cats.

I grew up in the most safety-conscious home God ever placed on planet Earth. Rick loves to tease me about the way my parents responded to safety "threats." When the sun went down each day, Rick says, the curtains were tightly closed, the doors were padlocked shut, the 8,000 watt motion-sensitive lights were activated, the moat in front of the house was filled with water, and the alligators were released to gobble up any intruder dumb enough to venture onto our property. OK, it was bad, but it wasn't *that* bad.

When I was in high school, I was voted the least likely to take a risk. (OK, it didn't really happen, but it could have.) I wanted to go to France as an exchange student for a semester, but my parents were fearful to let me go. They were afraid of what might happen to me if I went so far away. I have to be fair — we didn't have a lot of money, and that's probably the biggest reason they said no. But what I remember most is the fear they experienced when they contemplated my being part of any kind of adventure.

One of my most vivid childhood memories is seeing my dad at our kitchen table, poring over the plans for a bomb shelter that could be built in a basement. The Cold War was at its apex while I was in elementary school, and the idea that "the Russians are coming!" was on everyone's mind. My dad believed it too, hence the bomb shelter blueprints. The only problem was we lived in San Diego and nobody had a basement! I never did figure out where he thought he was going to put that thing.

But along with the fearful messages, I also received powerful messages about faith, risk, courage, and surrender. I had an elderly great-aunt who had been a missionary to China right before World War II broke out. When she would come to visit us, she would tuck me into bed and regale me with colorful snippets of her life: taking a freighter to China (no transpacific flights that quickly and effortlessly whisked one from Arizona to Shanghai in twelve hours); eating bird's nest soup and Peking Duck; watching women hobble around town on their tightly bound tiny feet; fearing the Japanese soldiers who appeared and began a reign of terror; and feeling deep sorrow at having to leave her adopted country and the people she had grown to cherish. She awakened in me a hunger to be on an adventure for God.

Marrying Rick Warren (risky, but it has turned out well!), moving two thousand miles away from all that was familiar to go to seminary, planting Saddleback Church with no money and no members — these have all been part of an adventure I have loved.

Eight years ago, God invited me to join him on the ride of my life, to go with him on an adventure unlike any I had ever been a part of before. When I said yes to his calling to become an advocate for persons infected and affected by HIV/AIDS and for orphans, my life became radically different.

I found myself — scaredy-cat Kay — taking risks, facing physical danger, and exposing myself to possible harm, not for gold medals, plaques to mount on the wall, or listings in

The Guinness Book of World Records, but for more eternal reasons. He didn't call me to scale mountains, ford streams, slay dragons, conquer uncharted lands, or strap myself to a rocket and launch into space. He called me to a very different type of adventure. The reality is, our physical world has been pretty thoroughly explored, charted, graphed, mapped, and conquered. But there is another world that is crying out for heroes, for people of adventure, for courageous leaders, for those willing to risk it all. It is the world of suffering, the world of fellow human beings in need, the world of global problems worthy of our greatest risks.

On my own journey of saying yes to God, I've witnessed the best and the worst this world offers. I've traveled to brothels and resorts, palaces and mud huts. Along the way I've met with presidents and prostitutes, billionaires and paupers. I've held newborn babies crying robustly and dying women whispering their last words.

This suffering world is in desperate need of heroes and unlikely heroes — chickens, wimps, scaredy-cats — who will nevertheless step out in faith and say "God, I'm scared to death, but I'm going to say yes to you."

In Deuteronomy 32:11, God is compared to a mother eagle that pushes her young to learn how to fly — "like an eagle that stirs up its nest and hovers over its young, that spreads its wings to catch them and carries them on its pinions."

Eagles don't build their nests in apricot trees or little bushes next to a road; they build them high on the sides of mountains, near the cliffs. Before the babies are born, the mother creates a soft, cushy environment for the eaglets to hatch and grow. She pads it with feathers and leaves. She arranges the sticks and twigs in such a way that it's a really comfortable place. But when it's time for those eaglets to learn how to fly, she begins to stir up the nest. She uses her beak and talons to rearrange those sticks and twigs so they start poking the eaglets. Instead of a comfy, cozy place, the nest is now quite uncomfortable. On top of that, she keeps nudging them over to the edge of the nest so they will be forced to jump out.

Of course, the eaglets don't think it's time for them to learn how to fly; they don't necessarily agree with mom's assessment of how things are going. From their perspective, she's nuts! "Excuse me — but have you looked over the side of this nest? There's an abyss down there! I'll die!" But as she keeps pushing the eaglet and prodding it, it ultimately has no choice but to jump. As it begins its free fall into what appears to be certain death, the mother eagle swoops down underneath and catches it on her wings, safely depositing it back in the nest. Then she stirs up the nest again, and the cycle starts over. She pushes it out of the nest, and its heart pounds furiously, certain it will die. Once again, she swoops underneath and catches it on her wings, safely depositing it back in the nest. This process is repeated until the bird learns how to fly.

Have you been in the nest too long? God may be using this book or your circumstances to stir up the nest of your life. It's starting to get uncomfortable? Good! Don't run; don't be afraid. It may look like an abyss below you, but you can be certain that God will do for you exactly what he has wired mother eagles to do. He will catch you; you will not fall. You can risk saying yes to God.

SURRENDER

Will you decide to say yes to God,
even before knowing the full implications
of what that yes may mean for you?

Father, you are disturbed by the misery you witness every day. None of it escapes your notice, but, honestly, a lot of it escapes mine. Forgive me for my complacency, my apathy, my ignorance. Help me to see the world through your eyes. I'm scared to surrender all to you; I'm not entirely sure I can trust you with what matters most to me. But I want to know you; I want to love like you love, and hurt the way you hurt. I want to live the adventure of risking it all for you. I am saying yes to you right now, no matter what that yes entails.

Prayer

SAY YES TO GOD

○ Begin to pray daily for God to open your eyes to new realities about yourself and your world.

○ Ask a friend to read this book with you. You'll benefit far more by discussing it, chapter by chapter, with a reading partner.

○ Listen to Kay's welcome message to you at www .kaywarren.com.

THE KINGDOM OF ME

*"Self-help is no help at all. Self-sacrifice is the way,
my way, to finding yourself, your true self."*
Luke 9:24 MSG

*Love is the way to maturity. Selfishness stunts growth
and keeps us in a spiritual playpen.*
Elisabeth Elliot, *A Lamp Unto My Feet*

WHEN I WAS ABOUT SIX YEARS OLD, MY DAD WENT ON A business trip and came back with the Disney record of the story of Cinderella. It quickly became one of my prized possessions, as I imagined myself as the beautiful servant girl who becomes a queen. I have vivid memories of making my little friends sit on the couch and watch me dance, twirling to the music of "A Dream Is a Wish Your Heart Makes." Notice I said "watch" me dance — they weren't allowed to participate at all! I did the singing, the dancing, the spinning, and the bowing — it was all about me. Forget about Prince Charming and Cinderella; it was the Kingdom of Kay.

Not much has changed.

I, like many other adults, devote a fair amount of time, energy, and money to controlling, polishing, protecting, and defending my own private little kingdom. Like a despotic ruler in a mythical story, I can be the omnipotent potentate, supreme authority, oppressive dictator, and highly exalted one in the Kingdom of Me. Of course, I would never say it out loud and might be outraged that anyone would even suggest that I operate that way, but it's the reality of the struggle I face every day. So do you. At my worst, I rule over my domain with an iron hand, fiercely protecting my territory, my possessions, my reputation, my persona, my dignity, my rights as queen. I am in control. As Gary Thomas observes, "The biggest block to our surrender is not our appetites and wayward desires but our addiction to running our own lives."[4]

Within this kingdom, there is very little room for anyone who doesn't do it my way, who doesn't agree that I am the most important person of all. When others treat me as I "deserve," then all is well — we can get along. When others acknowledge that it's right to serve me and my needs, there is harmony and peace. Woe to the hapless family member, friend, acquaintance, or stranger who doesn't properly appreciate my status; heads will roll. I relate completely to this quote from Fénelon: "Your self-love is terribly touchy. No matter how slightly it is insulted, it screams, 'Murderer.'"[5]

Not only do I seek complete control of everything around me, but my greatest and deepest love is reserved for me. I am desperately in love with myself. If I am completely honest, I have to admit that there are many times when I want the world to revolve around me — my comfort, my pleasure, my convenience. I desire that others see and interpret everything through *my* eyes, make *me* happy, meet *my* needs, and refrain from offending *me*, hurting *me*, wounding *me*, upsetting *me*, or irritating *me*. I want to be understood, appreciated, acknowledged, elevated, praised, valued, attended to, catered to, respected, admired, accommodated, listened to, loved, adored, and cherished.

My greatest efforts every day go toward myself. Even when I'm occupied with taking care of others, the meter is always running as I inwardly take notice of the hours I've spent, the energy I've expended, and the sacrifices I've made. I find myself gleeful when I am able to kill two birds (or more) with one stone by doing something for someone else (making myself look good) while doing something for me at the same time. At the end of the day, I do a final tally to see if others have done as much for me as I've done for them. If they haven't, then I am hurt, disappointed, frustrated, offended, demanding, and angry. Sometimes I withdraw from relationships because, according to my internal calculator, I'm giving more than I'm getting back.

Others-centered? Not often. Surrender control to someone else? Not a chance.

SURRENDERING THE KEYS TO THE KINGDOM

After God seriously disturbed me — shaking me up and yanking the blindfold off my eyes — I could see that I had some rearranging to do in my life. If I was going to begin to care about those who were infected and affected by HIV/AIDS, some things were going to have to change. However, I liked my life; it was comfortable, safe, predictable yet exciting — and on top of that, I had enough problems of my own.

Even though my initial response was to jump in with both feet, I began to think of all of the reasons I shouldn't get overly involved. Didn't I have enough to do? Wasn't there enough pressure in my life? Wasn't it enough of a challenge to keep my world aligned with my energetic husband's life? Didn't I have plenty of relationships to manage and nurture? Wasn't Saddleback a big enough project to keep my calendar full? What if I got sick? What if I became infected with the virus (HIV) that causes AIDS and died? I didn't want to be around sick people — they're depressing!

I was worried about my reputation. Since I erroneously thought that all HIV-positive people were homosexuals, how could I become an advocate for people with HIV without leading critics to believe that I had changed my theology of sexuality? In those early days of being disturbed, I didn't realize that even if my misperceptions were right — that everyone who has HIV is gay (not true; the majority of those infected around the world are women) — it wouldn't alter the appropriate response. I didn't yet understand that it is not a sin to be sick. I was just concerned that my reputation would suffer. A good reputation is hard to come by, and Rick and I had worked hard for more than twenty-two years to carefully guard our good name and our church's reputation. Years later, my attitude is completely different. I'm happy that my reputation includes caring for those whom many have rejected; but at the time, worrying about my reputation proved to be a crisis for me.

Besides, the problem was just too big. Why in the world would I suddenly decide that I had what it took to tackle the greatest humanitarian crisis of all time?

My reluctant thoughts may resonate with you. Are you asking yourself the same questions? As an eye-opening exercise, it may be helpful to make your own list of why you don't want to get too involved with people in their suffering — not just people with HIV, but anyone who is in need. When you come to the end of your reasons, I think you will find the same ugly reality I found: what stands in the way of your surrender to God's plan to engage with hurting people is simply that you care more about yourself than you do about the suffering of others.

What could ever break through those impossibly thick walls of self-centeredness? Who or what can change your perspective in such a way that instead of living to serve yourself, you actually *want* to live to serve someone else? To whom do we surrender the keys to the Kingdom of Me? A jailer? A torturer? A more powerful enemy who has beaten us into submission? A ruler whose intent is to ruin and destroy? No, we surrender to a Father who loves us unconditionally.

God wins us, not by shouting, beating us up, or starving us into submission, but by asking for an invitation to enter. We are *loved* into surrender. The more we accept that he operates out of love for us, the more we will entrust ourselves to him. Fénelon expresses this truth beautifully: "God is not a spy looking to surprise you. He is not an enemy lurking in the shadows to hurt you. God is your Father who loves you, and wants to help you if you will but trust in His goodness."[6]

The apostle Paul joyfully declares, "For [God the Father] has rescued us from the dominion of darkness and brought us into the kingdom of the Son he loves, in whom we have redemption, the forgiveness of sins" (Colossians 1:13 – 14). How does this happen? How do we move from the "dominion of darkness" into the "kingdom of the Son he loves"? How do we actually surrender the throne of the Kingdom of Me to that of the Kingdom of God?

The answer is simple but not easy. Once you begin to

catch a glimpse of the love that God has for you, you can relax in your attempts to manage your life by yourself. You acknowledge that God sent Jesus to mop up your messes — to pay the debt you owe for all of your failures. You believe by faith that Jesus did what he said he came to do — to give his life on your behalf — and then you accept his offer of salvation. You allow him to enter into your "kingdom" — your mind, will, and emotions — and take up residence there. The Kingdom of Me is now absorbed into *his* kingdom, and you will gradually allow Jesus to be at home there. Over time, you will experience the quiet confidence that comes from being a part of God's kingdom.

Scripture confirms that the more we recognize the love that compelled Jesus to pay the price for us to enter his kingdom, the more we will feel at home with him:

> I pray that from his glorious, unlimited resources he will empower you with inner strength through his Spirit. Then Christ will make his home in your hearts as you trust in him. Your roots will grow down into God's love and keep you strong. And may you have the power to understand, as all God's people should, how wide, how long, how high, and how deep his love is. May you experience the love of Christ, though it is too great to understand fully. Then you will be made complete with all the fullness of life and power that comes from God.
>
> *Ephesians 3:16 – 19 NLT*

As Jesus becomes more and more settled in us and our spiritual perspective grows, we become more willing to let him do the internal renovations necessary to make us more like him. We grow in our ability to become disciples, making surrender a more natural response.

WHAT THIS SURRENDER LOOKS LIKE

Once we surrender the keys to the Kingdom of Me to this loving Father, we are ready to give ourselves over to life in the Kingdom of God. Instead of cooperating with the firmly established rules in the Kingdom of Me — where we want God to pamper us and make our every wish come true — he asks us to surrender control and become a bond slave to Jesus in *his* kingdom. A bond slave is a person who *voluntarily* enters into the service of another. Voluntary surrender is the key. Jesus only comes in when asked, and he only assumes the leadership of my life when I voluntarily yield it to him. Every other moment of surrender to him grows from his initial invitation to join his kingdom. It's never easy. Giving up the rights to the Kingdom of Me goes against the grain of self, but it inevitably leads to a life beyond our wildest imagination. Not that fame, fortune, acclaim, or earthly reward comes to everyone — that's God's business to decide — but somewhere within each of us is a desire for significance, for meaning — a need to know that our time here on earth matters. This can only happen as we live as Jesus' bond slaves, voluntarily serving him in the places he leads us, whether far away or next door.

His invitation to join him is found in Mark 8:34: "Then [Jesus] called the crowd to him along with his disciples and said: 'If anyone would come after me, he must deny himself and take up his cross and follow me.'"

Imagine this scene with me. Jesus is talking to a crowd — nothing unusual about that. He was the kind of person who drew crowds because he regularly performed miracles. He multiplied pieces of bread and fish so that they could feed thousands, healed lepers, gave sight back to the blind, caused the deaf to hear, walked on water, cast out demons, and raised the dead. Some of them probably followed for the "wow factor" — seeking to be amused and amazed. Some saw him as an enemy to be dealt with. Probably most of those folks were just ordinary men and women in desperate need of a personal miracle, hoping that by getting close to Jesus some of what he was dishing out would rub off on them or their loved one. They followed him because of what he could do for them.

Jesus was well aware of the heart motivations of the hungry and thirsty people who would quickly assemble whenever he came to town; he never confused crowds with disciples. With that said, there's nothing wrong with starting out as a member of the crowd, as someone who is interested in Jesus because of his ability to heal broken minds and bodies, to fix things and make them right. But Jesus is intent on moving folks from the crowd into the core; he wants to turn crowds into disciples. On this particular day, he decides to challenge the crowd by drawing a vivid distinction between them, and those identified as his disciples. He doesn't leave anyone wondering at just what the distinction is. He gives three short qualifications for being his disciple: deny yourself, take up your cross, and follow him.

Denying Self

I don't know about you, but I'm instantly in trouble. *Deny myself?* I've already exposed the pathetic ways I look out for #1 a thousand times a day. It's not in my nature to deny myself. But that's the place Jesus starts in his definition of a disciple: someone who will say no to themselves and yes to

God. If you think you don't struggle here, go back and reread the first few pages of this chapter and see if you don't strongly identify with the subtle and not-so-subtle self-centered ways we operate.

You may be wondering why, if we already struggle with saying yes to God, I would make it even more challenging by adding the words *courageous* and *dangerous* to surrender. It's because of whom we surrender to. We don't surrender to a toothless, weak, powerless old man; we surrender to Almighty God — the Creator and Sustainer of the universe. He's God, for Pete's sake! And when you get close to God, *crazy stuff happens.* He has all the power; he's sovereign. Not only did he fling the stars into space, keep the planets in alignment, create you, and save you; he has the ability to take our lives and turn them upside down in the snap of a finger. We love it when God displays his power in miraculous ways that benefit us. We cheer wildly for God when our loved one is healed, when unexpected money flows our way and saves our bacon, when trouble is averted. We dance with delight when he is multiplying the fish and the loaves, healing the blind, raising the dead. That's the kind of God we want to be associated with. We're not so keen on God's power when circumstances seem to careen madly out of our control and he doesn't intervene. Suddenly, his authority and power seem frightening, and his insistence on being in control of the universe bumps squarely into my insistence that *I* be in control. Trouble brews.

Self-centeredness and "control issues" get in the way of saying yes to God. Through the years I've found an equally frustrating roadblock to denying myself and saying yes to God. That roadblock is *fear.*

Somewhere along the way, many people have developed a fear of God — being afraid of what he will allow in their lives or do to them if they ever truly surrender themselves to him. Can you identify with this fear? I remember the numerous times as a young mom when I lay in my bed in the middle of the night, anxiously worrying about my kids. I recall trying to bargain with God: "God, I really do love you, and I want to serve you with my whole heart. But I have to tell you, if you ever lay a finger on one of my kids, all bets are off." Ludicrous, isn't it? As if God was maliciously waiting for me to utter those fateful words "I surrender totally to you" so that he could unleash a torrent of pain and tragedy in response.

Where did this deep, visceral fear of God come from? All I can figure is that we assume a link between surrender and tragedy. Who can't name a friend or loved one who said a wholehearted yes to God, only to find the bottom fall out of their life almost instantaneously? We erroneously connect the two and conclude that saying yes to God brought evil into our lives. Our enemy has done a fantastic job of lying to us, convincing us that God is not *for* us, but *against* us.

This kind of thinking causes us to withhold parts of our hearts from God in an attempt to keep evil from happening; we end up trying to "protect" a dream, a vision, a person, a relationship from God, fearful he will take away the cherished thing if we surrender. We begin to play a spiritual game of "Deal or No Deal" with him. "Here's my deal for you, God. I'm going to serve you and love you and be yours, but I've got this dream. I'm not really sure you'll take care of it, so I'm going to hold it over here — out of your reach." Or "I love you, God, but I'm not sure you're going to let me be in that relationship so I'm going to withhold it from you so I can protect it. You leave it alone, and I'll serve you." We think we're serving God with passion and depth, but in reality, withholding parts of ourselves causes us to exist in an arm's-length distance relationship with him. It's almost impossible to be intimate with someone you don't trust.

Years ago, I heard Beth Moore talk about this tendency to withhold parts of ourselves from God because of our fear of what he will ask from us in response. Beth stated, "Evil will come because evil will come. But those who have withheld nothing from God will find that nothing separates them from God when evil comes."

The apostle John reminds us that "in this world [we] will have trouble" (John 16:33). If there's one ironclad guarantee in life, it is this: trouble will come. It wears a thousand different faces, but it comes to us all. No one escapes it. Because Adam and Eve's sinful choice to be their own god produced a broken planet where nothing works perfectly, evil touches all of us. We accuse God of cruelty in response to our surrender, but we are mistaken.

In The Chronicles of Narnia novels, C. S. Lewis depicts God as a majestic, magnificent lion, Aslan. One of the children in the story, Lucy, asks if this stately but intimidating lion is safe. "Safe?" said Mr. Beaver; "don't you hear what Mrs. Beaver tells you? Who said anything about safe? 'Course he isn't safe. But he's good. He's the King, I tell you."[7]

He's not a mild, tame deity who can be contained in a cage, so in that sense, he is definitely *not* "safe." But while God certainly has the power to turn our lives upside down — to move us from here to there in a heartbeat, his character is *always, unchangeably good.* Part of the soul work most of us need to do is to become utterly, irrevocably convinced from Scripture that he is good. If you build your life on the conviction that God is good and can be trusted, you won't be afraid to say yes to him in an act of courageous surrender; you won't hesitate to learn how to become adept at denying yourself.

Marriage has been one continuous opportunity for me to learn how to deny myself — not because Rick is harsh and demanding, but because two Kingdoms of Me can't exist peacefully in the same house. We discovered almost from the start that nearly every conflict we have has its roots in selfishness. It was so bad that on our honeymoon we memorized the verse "Only by pride cometh contention" (Proverbs 13:10 KJV)!

As much as I hate to admit it, my self-centeredness has driven me to argue, to be defensive, to guard my turf, and to say mean things to Rick. When my feelings are hurt or I am angry, I am tempted to let loose with sarcastic comments and statements designed to wound him. I'm not always interested in doing the right thing in those moments. Denying myself and what I want is excruciatingly difficult. Of course, in the thick of conflict, I can't always see what is behind my behavior, but when I step back and calmly analyze it, I can usually identify my efforts to prop up and maintain my own kingdom. Looking back over more than three decades of marriage, I see that I've wasted a ton of emotional energy on meaningless arguments. In the heat of the moment, what kind of bath soap to use has felt like a life-and-death issue, but in the grand scheme of my life with Rick, it's surely not worth fighting about.

We're slow learners, but we're coming to the place where loving each other is more important than being "right." In the movie *The Princess Bride*, the lowly peasant who serves the princess acquiesces to her every request with the phrase "as you wish." In fact, when they meet again later in the story after a long separation, it is his repetition of these words that causes her to recognize him. I'm practicing that simple phrase. I don't always say it out loud, but my heart is turned toward Rick, allowing me to choose to seek his best interests rather than my own. "You want to blast the car's air-conditioning on a winter day? As you wish." "You would like to watch this dumb TV show? As you wish." "You would like to change the dates of the family vacation? As you wish."

Please don't misunderstand my point. I'm not suggesting that only the woman in a marriage has to give up her wants and desires. Not at all! Scripture makes no apology for instructing wives *and* husbands to show honor and respect to each other in a relationship of mutuality (see Ephesians 5:21). I'm speaking of my personal journey and how I'm learning to pause and consider whether my desires for personal comfort can be presented instead as an offering of love to Jesus. Can I deny myself? Can I say no to myself?

Do I get it right every time? Not on your life. Honoring someone else's desires and wishes over my own is a slow death to self. But it's the beginning step in learning how to be a disciple. The first part of Jesus' invitation — "deny yourself" — lies at the heart of courageous surrender.

Taking Up the Cross

Again, picture the scene in Mark 8 with me. This time, Jesus has captured the attention of this crowd, not with his miracles, but with his words. He begins to ratchet up the requirement for being a disciple. Not only do I have to learn how to deny myself and say yes to God; he says I must take up a cross.

I have heard dozens of sermons on Mark 8:34 and read all sorts of commentaries on this passage. Most of the time, pastors and scholars seem hesitant to take this verse at face value; they usually attempt to strip it of its punch in the gut and spiritualize it, seeking a principle hidden in the stark command. And realistically, it makes sense to take the richness of the spiritual principle of dying to self and apply it to our daily lives since few of us will ever have to face a literal cross.

Every day, God gives us opportunities to "take up our crosses" and die to ourselves through the circumstances that come our way. While the circumstances themselves are not crosses, the way in which we navigate through them becomes the proving ground. For instance, waiting for physical healing that doesn't happen, living for years with a mentally ill loved one, watching a child die, hoping to have a child but never experiencing it, dreaming of a career that never takes off, longing for an intimacy never quite achieved, struggling to make ends meet, seeking friendships that don't disappoint, bearing the rejection of society because you are sick — these are opportunities to prove whether or not we will be obedient to God.

We can all take the "curse God and die" approach of Job's wife (Job 2:9), or we can adopt Job's approach: "The LORD gave and the LORD has taken away; may the name of the LORD be praised" (Job 1:21). We can decide that we will no longer serve him if he doesn't take the pain away. We can conclude that he doesn't understand our longing for a fulfilling marriage and repudiate our vows and search for someone else. We can reason that he doesn't really know what he's talking about when he says that sexual purity is for our own good, and then decide to throw away his standards. Or we can choose to listen to him, honor him, respect his commands, and obey him at any cost, no matter how hard the "dying" becomes. This is how we grow into spiritual maturity. Without the opportunity to die every day, we will remain spiritual babies. If we're not presented with the option of choosing self over him, we will never become like Jesus in our character. He chose the Father's will, not his own, time after time and became our ultimate model of courageous surrender. It was his courageous surrender that allowed him to take up his cross.

I've already told you about the momentous day when I finally understood that God had chosen me to be an ordinary person and when I began to celebrate his sovereign design. It changed my view of God, of myself and my place in the world, and of Rick. It created in me an expectation that someday God would use me for his good purposes. I began to wait for my turn to shine.

The days turned into months, the months into years.

Rick became a well-known Christian leader as our church exploded with growth. Publishers wanted to publish his books. Speaking opportunities came a mile a minute. Magazines and radio stations wanted interviews. It seemed as though he was receiving recognition and awards on a daily basis. Everyone wanted him.

While he was thriving in the spotlight, I was withering on the vine. Not only was he receiving all of the attention, but family situations seemed to take me even further away from being used by God. One of our children had some severe biochemical challenges and needed an extraordinary amount of parenting; I gradually resigned from most of my ministry roles to be available. Rick and I shared the nurturing role, but he was still able to maintain his active ministry as my focus became narrower and narrower.

Then Rick's father became ill with cancer. As a widower, he depended on his children to care for him. Rick's brother, Jim, and his sister, Chaundel, and her husband, Tom, shared the responsibility with us of helping Rick's dad through his last years of his life. Those months were filled with hospitalizations, surgeries, treatments, and finally home care. Family came first for me, so there were no big agonizing decisions to make about how to spend my time; but I ended up feeling more and more as if I had been set on a shelf. Rick constantly encouraged me with affirmation and did his best to create opportunities that would allow me to use my gifts, but the circumstances of my life just didn't allow for much ministry.

I began to be envious of my husband — not the short-lived feelings of jealousy that disappear as quickly as they come, but the settled-in emotion of envy that began to rot my bones. I remember sitting on our couch one evening staring at nothing in particular. Rick had just excitedly told me about *another* magazine that wanted him to write an article, but instead of being happy for him, my heart had gone cold: "When will it be my turn, God? Don't I have anything to say that's worth listening to? Will anybody ever care about *my* ideas?" That's when it hit me — I was envious of my husband. I had stopped being Rick's cheerleader and become a critic. I was no longer rejoicing in his victories and successes but resenting the lack of them in my life. It's painful and embarrassing to admit my sin, but it's the truth. The Kingdom of Me was on display in full force.

To be honest, it scared me. I didn't *want* to feel bitter and envious of Rick; it made us strangers instead of partners. After he went to bed that night, I analyzed my predicament, horrified at the ugliness in my soul. I journaled for hours and took another step into courageous surrender as I prayed this prayer:

> God, if you want me to be at the back of the line while Rick is at the front of the line, so be it. If you choose to give him all the attention and fame, and nobody ever knows my name, that's OK with me. If the best way I can serve you is to create a safe haven in our home for my husband so that he can be more effective, I'll do it. If your plan for my life is not to be a public speaker or an author but to raise my beautiful children to love you and serve you so that their lives have a far greater impact than either me or Rick — that's what I want. I don't care anymore. If taking up the cross to serve you means being put on the shelf indefinitely or even forever, I'm yours.

Prayers of surrender have the power to radically alter the course of our lives. I have no doubt that if I had not decided to surrender — to take up the cross of self-denial — my marriage would have begun to deteriorate. I would have grown increasingly bitter toward and resentful of Rick, which would have led to friction and conflict. I would have seen him as an enemy to undermine rather than a partner to build up. My spiritual life with Jesus would have suffered if I had angrily accused him of neglecting me. But saying "as you wish" to God and daily taking up the cross of denying my desires for a vibrant personal ministry led to serenity. Suddenly I was released from comparing myself to Rick. I could be genuinely happy about the opportunities that came his way and could share his excitement. I stopped fretting over what would happen to me; any gifts I had were given to me by God, and if he chose to use them in a way that was different from the way I wanted them to be used, that was his decision. I was finally at peace.

Surrender *always* leads to peace. Accepting God's will in our circumstances is the hardest thing he asks of us because it requires denying ourselves and taking up the cross. If we forget that it is to a loving God that we surrender the keys to the Kingdom of Me, we will struggle long and hard against him. The good news is that his arms are around us, and we can beat our fists against his chest for as long as we like. But what *rest* for our souls comes when we finally relax into his embrace! Fénelon makes this observation:

> God prepares a cross for you that you must embrace without thought of self-preservation. The cross is painful. Accept the cross and you will find peace even in the middle of turmoil. Let me warn you that if you push the cross away, your circumstances will become twice as hard to bear. In the long run, the pain of resisting the cross is harder to live with than the cross itself.[8]

I get it. I get how important it is to view my life from the perspective of dying to myself. I don't always like it, but I get it. At the same time, I can't help but wonder if Jesus didn't also mean *exactly what he said*. There was no such thing in those days as a cross tattoo or a piece of jewelry on a leather strap or a crocheted bookmark. No spectacular paintings or sculptures of crosses; no wooden and metal wall hangings. A cross only had one purpose: a cruel death for the person nailed to it.

I can envision Jesus glancing over his shoulder as he spoke to the crowd and seeing a man carrying a wooden cross to his own crucifixion. I wonder if he turned back to the crowd and said, "If you want to be mine — if you want to move from being a member of the crowd to being a disciple — you must learn what it means to take up a cross. You must be willing to give your life for me if I ask you to."

I'll talk more about this in a later chapter, but before he came to earth, Jesus had been in the perfection of heaven. He saw my sin and degradation and knew there was no chance I could do anything on my own to restore the broken relationship that existed between me and the Father. My condition disturbed him. It disturbed him to the point that he was willing to leave the comfort and delight of heaven to be with me … to suffer for me … to take up *his* cross.

We shouldn't think it strange, then, that he would ask us to do the same thing. Men and women who become seriously disturbed by all that is wrong in this world will deny themselves to the point that they are willing to give their own lives if God asks them to do so.

When I became an advocate for people living with HIV/AIDS, I was completely ignorant about the virus and how it was transmitted. I had heard it was easy to spread HIV, so I was very concerned that I might become HIV positive myself. Saying yes to becoming an advocate meant confronting my anxiety about getting sick. I remember praying, "God, I believe you have called me to care for sick people; if in doing so, I become HIV positive myself, and even die of AIDS, I'm willing to do that. If my death leads to others knowing that you love them and died for them, then my life is yours."

I quickly learned that my fears were needless and unfounded; unlike the common cold virus, HIV is quite difficult to transmit. Casual contact with an infected person has zero risk of infection for me. But I didn't know it at the time. My prayer was sincere and from the heart. I was as willing as I've ever been to lay down my life, to take up the cross for Jesus' sake.

What disturbs you enough to even begin to consider taking up a cross in Jesus' name?

Following Jesus

After calling us to the radical discipleship of denying ourselves and taking up the cross, Jesus invites us to follow him. At first glance, the meaning of this command seems incredibly vague and hard to pin down. Does following Jesus mean we are all supposed to take vows of silence, poverty, and celibacy? Do we all have to sell everything we own, live in a commune, give up our cars, and wear odd, mismatched clothes? Are we supposed to stop watching television and going to movies, burn our secular music CDs, disconnect the Internet, and grow our own food? Is the goal of following Jesus Christ to disengage and withdraw from life as we know it? Through the centuries, God has certainly led some of his devoted followers to make personal decisions that are at odds with mainstream culture, but while this may be the experience of a few, most of us don't hear God's prompting to go to such extremes.

So if following Christ isn't ultimately about where we live, what we wear, or whether or not we have a television set, what *does* it mean to follow Jesus in a life-altering way? This is a topic we'll explore more fully in the next chapter, but I can give you a glimpse of what following Jesus has looked like in my life.

The undeveloped photograph began to take some form and shape. As I learned more about HIV/AIDS, I realized that God was asking me to be an advocate for those infected and affected, to speak up on their behalf. I couldn't see around the bend to know what was ahead. I couldn't see where the road would lead, what roadblocks I'd find in the way, and what it would cost to follow him. I had taken the gigantic leap of faith that said yes to him without knowing what that surrender entailed. Like Indiana Jones in *Indiana Jones and the Last Crusade*, I had stepped off the cliff into what could be a bottomless abyss, only to find that there was a stable structure underneath me. I had to trust that while I couldn't see where the steps of faith were leading me, I was walking on a firm structure that wouldn't let me fall. That's what it means to follow Jesus — saying yes and trusting that he won't let us fall, even when we can't see exactly where he's leading.

An earlier experience with God had paved the way for me to trust him. For the first thirteen years of our church, we had no permanent building. We used high school gyms for worship services and bank buildings, homes, and community centers for meetings during the week. Each weekend, we hauled trailers full of nursery and sound equipment to the school, where volunteers set them up and then took them down hours later. Every toy, crib, rocking chair, changing table, craft project, microphone, speaker, music stand, keyboard, coffeepot, name tag, and pencil had to go in a trailer — a process that was repeated every weekend for thirteen years.

Land is astronomically expensive in Southern California,

and we didn't have the financial resources to buy a piece of property for our burgeoning congregation. Time and time again, we would locate a piece of property and ask our members to give sacrificially and to pray, only to watch the deal fall through for a variety of reasons. Rick always took the delays and disappointments in stride, but I struggled to maintain an optimistic attitude. Certainly we believed that in God's timing, our church would have a permanent home. But eventually it got *so old*.

One evening Rick came home from work and informed me that although we had finally purchased a piece of land, the county supervisors would not approve the building permits because of newly discovered environmental issues. We were delayed again — indefinitely.

"That's it!" I yelled at him. "I'm sick and tired of this stupid game. You've been too nice to those county supervisors. Let *me* go down to their offices and go nose to nose with them — I'll make them cough up the approval!" I was furious. Rick, never one to antagonize an angry woman, backed away. I stormed out of the living room, went into our home office, and slammed the door. I looked up at the ceiling and shook my fist at God and began to rant and rave: "What do you want from us? Haven't we tried to do things the way you want us to do them? Haven't we tried to follow you? Haven't we had integrity and honesty in our business dealings? Haven't we exercised faith and trust in you? I don't get it — just tell us what you want us to do, and stop messing with us!"

If my tirade wasn't already over the top, I then changed the argument into accusations of favoritism: "Why does Bill Hybels have acres of land for Willow Creek, and we don't?

Why did you give Chuck Smith and Calvary Chapel land and buildings? Why does Adrian Rogers's church in Tennessee have land? They just bought two hundred acres! What do they need two hundred acres for? We don't have any land, and they've got two hundred stinkin' acres! You just don't care about us."

It's a wonder that God didn't strike me dead on the spot; the accusations I hurled at him were vicious. I was almost out of my mind with anger, bitterness, frustration, and hurt. My passionate outburst soon left me spent and empty. I sank into the chair in our office, put my head on the desk, and wept in total defeat.

After I had lain there for a while, my arms sprawled on the desk, I noticed my Bible lying within reach. As mad as I was, I knew there was nowhere else to go but to God. I flipped randomly through the pages until I came to John 21. I had taught on this passage of Scripture that week in a Bible study, but I had missed the personal application to my life. Now it stared me in the face.

In one of his postresurrection appearances to his disciples, Jesus has a riveting encounter with Peter. Jesus asks Peter three times in a row if he loves him. Peter responds affirmatively each time, increasingly agitated and hurt because Jesus doesn't seem to believe him. Suddenly Jesus changes the tone of the conversation, almost as if to say, "OK — if you really mean it, then let me tell you what loving me will lead to":

> "I tell you the truth, when you were younger you dressed yourself and went where you wanted; but when you are old you will stretch out your hands, and someone

else will dress you and lead you where you do not want to go." Jesus said this to indicate the kind of death by which Peter would glorify God. Then he said to him, "Follow me!"

Peter turned and saw that the disciple whom Jesus loved was following them. (This was the one who had leaned back against Jesus at the supper and had said, "Lord, who is going to betray you?") When Peter saw him, he asked, "Lord, what about him?"

Jesus answered, "If I want him to remain alive until I return, what is that to you? You must follow me."

John 21:18 – 22

With no apologies, Jesus bluntly tells Peter that he will die for his faith. No comforting words, no pats on the back, no softening of the shocking prediction here. In fact, Jesus' next words issue Peter the hardest challenge he has ever faced: "Follow me. You're going to die, Peter, but first I want you to follow me."

Peter does what most of us would do. He turns and scans the group of disciples gathered around them, looking for a friendly face, and says, "Yeah? Well, what about *him*? What's going to happen to John? You got any shocking news to deliver to *him* today?"

These next words are the ones that shattered my argument with God. Jesus puts an end to any potential protests — "It's not fair!" "You've got favorites." "You love him more than you love me!" He simply says, "Peter, if I want John to remain alive until I come back, what is that to you? *You* follow me."

As I sat at that desk, exhausted from my railings against God, he spoke to me through his Word: "Kay, it's none of your business what I allow in another church. If I let every church on the face of the earth have land and buildings and Saddleback never does, what is that to you? Will you still follow me?"

Yes, Lord. Yes.

You see, it really *isn't* any of my business — or your business — what God does in someone else's life. My only business is to *follow him*. I sometimes call this the WITTY principle — **w**hat **is** **t**hat **t**o **y**ou? We wrongly accuse God of having favorites, of loving others more than he loves us, of showering others with blessings while leaving us high and dry. We pray and ask for a miracle in our family, only to watch things crumble around us. Yet a friend prays for a miracle in her family and seems to get one. We beg God to heal someone we love, but he or she dies anyway. Another friend asks God to heal their loved one — and he does. We conclude that there is an inequity to his love, and some choose to walk away from him.

Here's the bottom line: Figuring out God's ways isn't any of my business. Following him is.

Following Jesus is to offer to him all that you think you are, all that you really are, all that you think you are not, and all that you really are not — to be used in the way he chooses. It is stepping down from the throne in the Kingdom of Me and joining a new kingdom — the Kingdom of God. It's following him, even when following makes no sense. I'm not there yet, but I'm on my way.

I've taped to my desk an old Puritan prayer from the 1600s, and I read it nearly every day. I repeat it loudly and joyfully on my good days; on my bad days I force it through gritted teeth. On the terrible days I whisper a few of the words — and on the days when it all just seems like a big cosmic joke, I gaze through my tears at heaven and let my spirit speak to his with no words at all.

The Covenant Prayer

I am no longer my own, but yours.
Put me to what you will, rank me with whom you will;
put me to doing, put me to suffering;
let me be employed for you or laid aside for you,
exalted for you or brought low for you;
let me be full, let me be empty;
let me have all things, let me have nothing;
I freely and heartily yield all things to your pleasure
    and disposal.
And now, O glorious and blessed God, Father, Son
    and Holy Spirit,
you are mine, and I am yours.
So be it.
And the covenant which I have made on earth,
let it be ratified in heaven.
Amen.*

Now is the time for you to step down from the throne of the Kingdom of Me and become a part of the Kingdom of God, to become voluntary servants of the God who made you and loves you. His way is not always easy, but it leads to peace.

---

* John Wesley introduced this prayer into Methodism in 1755 and credited it to the seventeenth-century Puritan Richard Alleine. The version quoted here is updated with more contemporary language.

SURRENDER

Will you voluntarily surrender the keys
to the Kingdom of Me and accept
Jesus' dangerous invitation to deny yourself,
take up your cross, and follow him?

Prayer

God, what you ask of me seems beyond my reach.
I know I'm too protective of the Kingdom of Me.
Part of me is ready to start living more for you
than for myself, but part of me is desperately
afraid. Please forgive me for living for myself.
I've gotten really good at it. I see more and more
clearly now that surrendering to you — denying
myself, taking up the cross, and following you — is
going to cost me. But because I know you made
me out of your great love for me and you gave
yourself for me, I am handing you the keys to the
Kingdom of Me. Save me from myself.

SAY YES TO GOD

○ Right now, take a few minutes to identify the most common situations in which you personally struggle with the Kingdom of Me. If you have a reading partner, share your reflections the next time you meet.

○ Memorize Mark 8:34 – 37: "Then [Jesus] called the crowd to him along with his disciples and said: 'If anyone would come after me, he must deny himself and take up his cross and follow me. For whoever wants to save his life will lose it, but whoever loses his life for me and for the gospel will save it. What good is it for a man to gain the whole world, yet forfeit his soul? Or what can a man give in exchange for his soul?'"

○ Check out the Ego Assessment at www.kaywarren.com for deeper insight.

GLORIOUSLY RUINED

My children, our love should not be just words and talk;
it must be true love, which shows itself in action.
1 John 3:18 GNB

Throughout history, an authentic faith has been
marked by a compassionate response
toward those the world tends to forget.
Gary Thomas, *Authentic Faith*

OVER THE NEXT YEAR FOLLOWING MY DECISION TO SUR-render to God's call, I grew restless to see the HIV/AIDS pandemic in Africa with my own eyes, to somehow make the staggering statistics real. Just learning about HIV/AIDS from books, videos, websites, medical personnel, and relief organizations wasn't enough. I didn't yet understand that HIV/AIDS was a problem in America — it was an article on AIDS in Africa that had caught my attention, and so Africa became my focus. I *had* to go to Africa. Almost exactly a year to the date after God had seriously disturbed me about HIV/AIDS, I found myself on a plane headed to Mozambique, a country on the southeastern coast of Africa.

My journal entry on March 18, 2003, recorded my thoughts as I headed into an unknown future:

I wonder how many of these trips I will make. Why are there tears rolling down my face? How can I describe the myriad of emotions — from the most mundane and self-centered to the most sacrificial and loving emotions I am capable of?

Father, I am vaguely aware of the magnitude of what I don't know as this season of my life begins. It's inevitable that I will look back and laugh at my naïveté, my innocence, and my rash actions, judgments, and thoughts, but in the process, may I not wound others as I find my way. I pray that no one else has to suffer because I was blind, stubborn, foolish, or misguided. As much as I know how, I ask you to shatter my illusions, tear down my kingdoms, reveal my own heart and motives, and destroy all that is not of you in my life. Most of all, I want to know you to the limits that my humanity can handle. I'm waiting anxiously for THAT DAY when knowing you will be as familiar and effortless as taking a breath.

The Polaroid picture of what God was doing in my life was still mostly gray and blurry; I could only discern the outlines of the shapes that were beginning to develop. Even so, I had an inkling that I was on an adventurous journey that would include growing in intimacy with God. Somehow I sensed that the promise of knowing him in deeper and more extraordinary ways was inherent in my surrender to becoming an advocate for people with HIV/AIDS.

ON THE WAY

One of the major Christian relief organizations, World Relief, heard about my interest in AIDS and offered to host me in Mozambique, where they had developed a strong work. Three of us — the local representative from World Relief, my friend Marlene, and I — boarded a plane in Los Angeles with a final destination of Maputo, Mozambique. As I sat in the 747's window seat, looking down at the tarmac, it occurred to me that none of the airport crew members scurrying to finish their tasks had any idea of how momentous this flight was for me in my journey of surrender to God's agenda. I wanted to shout it out to everyone: "I'm going to Africa!"

I had heard a lot about Africa throughout my life. Visiting missionaries held me spellbound with tales of a land where monkeys, elephants, and lions roamed. A small elephant carved from ebony with ivory tusks sat on my father's desk as a memento from a missionary to Kenya. While I was captivated by the adventurous parts of missionary encounters, I also was a little frightened by the stories of difficult service on "the Dark Continent." Like many others of my generation, I had come to the erroneous conclusion that if you totally surrendered your life to God, he might send you to Africa. All of my friends prayed that God would send them anywhere except that dreaded place. I'm not sure why being sent to Africa represented total surrender to us when I was a kid. I can think of a few reasons, most of which have to do with ignorance, prejudice, and superstition.

But Africa was ground zero for AIDS, so it was to Africa I would go.

MEETING JOANNA AND FLORA

The twenty-hour plane trip was uneventful, although my mind and heart were racing. We arrived in the evening, and as we landed, I could see thousands of small cooking fires dotting the landscape. The air was heavy with heat, humidity, and smoke from the fires. I slept well once we arrived at the hotel and woke up on my first morning with a sense that something was about to happen that would change my life. Here's what I wrote in my journal:

> *What will this day hold? This day is fragile. It is sacred. There will never be another "first day in Africa" again. What do you want from me today, Father? Clean hands, a pure heart, obedience, trust — these are things I'm certain of before another moment unfolds.*

I couldn't decide if I was more scared or excited. Nothing looked familiar, and for the first time in my life, I was in the minority. All of the people around me were various shades of black, and I was white — not tan, but white! I wanted to be inconspicuous while I got acclimated to Mozambique and not be noticed if I happened to do something stupid, but there was no hiding! I was immediately an object of interest and curiosity. Children, not hampered by social mores, openly stared, giggled, and pointed. I'm fairly certain that many of them commented on my pasty, colorless skin tone and weird yellow hair. "What is all that paint on her face?" they must have asked each other.

My hosts from World Relief were eager to take me to meet men and women who were HIV positive. We piled into old Land Rovers with bench seats that allowed us to look at each other as we drove. I plied them with questions, but they were wise enough to ask me to just observe and listen to the people I met. They told me that in time I would begin to understand; I figured they thought most of my questions were ignorant and going down the wrong trail, but they were kind. We bumped along dirt roads dotted with huge pot- holes, our bodies swaying and moving in harmony with the jarring jolts from the rutted ground. Before long, we parked and then walked through low greenery toward a tree with spreading limbs.

At first, a faded piece of fabric was all I could see.

Under the canopy of leaves, the piece of fabric turned out to be a dying, homeless woman named Joanna. I was told that when people in her village learned that she and her husband had AIDS, the villagers asked them to leave. A distant relative offered to care for her and her husband, and so they moved. But when their new neighbors heard their diagnosis, the tiny straw hut they had built was mysteriously burned. The day I met her, Joanna was living under the large tree. She had no shelter, no cooking pots, no blankets, no extra clothes — just a sheet of plastic to lie on. She saw us approaching on foot and made a valiant effort to pick herself up off the ground to greet us, but with unrelenting diarrhea and an emaciated body, she was unable to stand. She crawled toward us on her elbows and knees. At one point, she col- lapsed in a heap, and her auntie scrambled to lift her onto the piece of plastic, which served as a welcome mat for the visitors. Joanna arranged her thin body in a dignified pose and waited to greet us. She was just a bag of bones.

I was stunned.

I know how to talk to people who are stressed about their

careers, discouraged with their parenting, upset because they can't lose the weight they want to. But nothing, absolutely nothing, in my experience or my faith had prepared me to speak to a homeless woman dying of AIDS and living under a tree. I smiled on the outside, but on the inside I was in a total panic — angry at God, angry at the brokenness of our world, searching the dim recesses of my mind for something halfway spiritual to say. I choked; I couldn't come up with anything other than "My name is Kay; thank you for your hospitality to us."

Fortunately, Debbie Dortzbach, international HIV director for World Relief and my host, *was* experienced. She had seen hundreds of women like Joanna, and her faith was strong. She showed me how to greet Joanna with warmth and kindness, how to kneel down next to her and look her in the eye, how to place my arms around her and hug her, how to pray and ask for God's comfort, strength, and help to be given in this terrible situation. She spoke of the hope of heaven — that while this world held pain and sorrow and sickness for Joanna, there is a better world she could be a part of through faith in Jesus, who loves her. Debbie offered a few antinausea pills that she carried with her to alleviate some of the discomfort Joanna was feeling, but even as inexperienced as I was, I knew this woman was only days away from death.

I left Joanna under that tree, but she remains with me. Her picture hangs on the wall of my office, and I look at her every day. She gave AIDS a name; she gave it a face.

I could have gone home after the first day; I had enough experiences to occupy my mind and heart for years to come. But there were more people to meet and love, more scenes to disturb me.

Flora lived in a tiny house, but at least it was a house. She cried softly as she told me her story. Her husband had an affair and got his mistress pregnant. He discovered that he was HIV positive, his mistress was HIV positive, and their newborn baby was HIV positive. Then Flora found out that she was HIV positive as well; her husband's unfaithfulness had brought HIV home. To add insult to injury, her unfaithful husband insisted that his mistress and her baby move into the tiny house with him, Flora, and their three children. When I met her, Flora was living in that dreadful situation.

Once again my faith had not prepared me to minister to anyone facing the challenges she faced. I managed to croak out the words "How can I pray for you? I'm going back to my country, and I would like to tell my friends about you. What can I ask them to pray for?"

I expected her to say, "Pray that my rat of a husband kicks his mistress out of my house," or "Please ask your friends to send me some money for medication," or "Would you ask them to pray that I get well?" Instead, she made the heart-rending request I've heard repeated by mothers around the world: "Would you ask them to pray for my children? Who will take care of them? No one will want them when they find out I've died of AIDS." I had no words, nothing meaningful to say. I couldn't promise that she would live or that her children would be welcomed by a neighbor or family member who would value and love them. I smiled again on the outside while my emotions churned inside.

When I returned to Orange County, my friends and family members asked me, "How was your trip? What was it like?" I stumbled to find the right words to describe it, but I didn't do a very good job. There was nothing in my life as an American that prepared me for what I had seen in rural Africa. Nothing. I kept trying to come up with comparisons: "Think of _____; it's sort of like that, but not really." I had never seen such poverty, such sickness, and such a lack of the basic necessities of life. No running water, no toilets, little or no electricity; few cars, a few banged-up bicycles; torn and mismatched clothes, no shoes, meager food — nothing that resembled life as I knew it.

GOING BACK

As disturbed as I was by my first trip to Africa to learn about HIV, I was hungry to learn more. Six weeks later, I visited two other African countries — Malawi and South Africa — with another Christian relief organization, World Vision. Again, the same intense heat beat down on us. Mountains that rose in asymmetrical peaks looked completely foreign to my eyes — ancient volcanoes shrouded in mist. Everywhere I looked, women were walking, most of them barefoot. Each carried a baby on her back, along with a five-gallon jug of water on her head; most carried firewood or charcoal as well.

In a rural area of Malawi, I walked through a village of circular mud huts with straw roofs to visit a CHH — initials that represent the sterile, clinical designation "Child-Headed Household," a euphemism for "orphans." Fifteen-year-old John was both father and mother to his eleven-year-old brother, George, and his three-year-old baby sister, Nisende. Their father and mother had died of AIDS. This part of Malawi wasn't accustomed to seeing many white visitors, so with my pale skin, blonde hair, and light blue eyes, I looked dead to them! John and his brother were polite but somber; the little sister never smiled. They proudly showed us the interior of their mud hut — a tiny room with a couple of tattered blankets and a dented cooking pot. As I sat on the mud porch of their hut, I coaxed the little girl to sit on my lap for a picture. If you look closely at the picture I have on my wall, you'll see that although I am smiling, my eyes are filled with tears.

I wanted nothing more than to fall on the ground and scream and sob — wailing to God on this little girl's behalf. All I could see was a future without the guiding love and support of the parents who had brought her into the world. Where was the daddy who would be her protector? Where was the father who would swing her into the air and listen for her squeals of delight? Where was the daddy who would stand proudly at her wedding, giving her in marriage? Where was the mommy who would cuddle her in the night and sing her back to sleep when she had a bad dream? Where was the mommy who would teach her how to be a woman? I barely contained my sobs until I got back to our van, where I cried and cried. My friend and colleague Elizabeth and I clung to each other in terrible grief.

Being seriously disturbed was becoming a way of life.

The grinding, relentless poverty made me cry. The orphaned children captured my heart and squeezed it until I thought it would burst. The women infected with HIV by faithless husbands stunned me with their courage. The men, baffled by and chagrined because of their increasingly weak bodies, made me ache for lives cut short. Day by day, the weight of their pain pushed me closer and closer to despair.

Then it was time to go home.

BRINGING AFRICA HOME

If very little in my life had prepared me for what I experienced in Africa, nothing had prepared me to try to pick up my life again in affluent Orange County, California. Everything looked different; everyone seemed strange. I looked at my possessions differently. Suddenly a full refrigerator was an insult. The crowded grocery store shelves were excessive. The displays of fashion at the mall were trivial. Television was disgusting and moronic. Politics made me sick. Church was superficial. I was a mess.

Elizabeth wrote me an email shortly after we got back from Malawi and South Africa. In it she told me, "Thanks a lot! I'm ruined — gloriously ruined." I nodded with sudden understanding. "That's it — that describes what has happened to me." I was ruined for life as I had known it before, but *gloriously* ruined! Life will always hold a "Before AIDS" and an "After AIDS" classification for me now. I'm simply not the person I used to be, although who I was before wasn't a bad person. But I've been shaped by these new experiences, and I will never be the same. Moreover, I don't *want* to be the same. I can't have seen what I've seen, met the people I've met, experienced what I've experienced, only to turn away and return to life as usual. I now look at life through a different set of lenses.

I am convinced that the unrestrained pursuit of the American Dream — health, wealth, and happiness — in and of itself can ruin you. The landscape is littered with the wounded from the ruined relationships, marriages, and families of driven men and women in feverish pursuit of the American Dream. Maybe you know this story all too well. Where has the pursuit of health, wealth, and happiness taken you? What price have you paid to achieve financial security, stability, or success? Who or what has been ruined along the way? Let's move the discussion from the theoretical to the intensely practical for a minute. Gals, I love shoes as much as the next woman, but how many pairs of shoes can you own before it starts to feel a little hollow? Guys, how many electronic gadgets can you possess before it all starts to feel just a little bit empty?

If the pursuit of the American Dream can ruin you, so can following Jesus Christ to the end of radical discipleship. But if I'm going to be ruined, I want to be ruined for something of eternal value; I want to be ruined for something that lasts. I want to be ruined for the Kingdom of God.

As I have grappled with how to live out this "ruined" life and still maintain healthy daily living, I have discovered that I actually live in three worlds — all of which are real. There is my world, the suffering world, and the spiritual world. The first one is where I make my living and raise my family; it is a world of supermarkets, malls, affluence, and plenty. It's the day-to-day world in which I interact with family, neighbors, coworkers, fellow church members, and people in my community. This is the world in which I have to make my faith real, not just theoretical.

In my world, I came back from trips to Africa convinced that it was hypocritical for me to weep for HIV-positive people thousands of miles away and to care nothing for those infected in my own community. As a result, I started the HIV/AIDS Initiative at Saddleback Church. A small band of men and women responded eagerly to my first message on AIDS, and we began to meet regularly to figure out what we could do to make a dent in the pandemic in our part of the world. There were men, women, and children infected and affected in Orange County, but we didn't know who they were. Our church was not a safe place for people to disclose their HIV status at that time. Other than two nurses, none of us had any medical background or training; none had traveled extensively to Africa or anywhere else; none understood the complexities of the way HIV affects lives. We were basically ignorant. We were low on knowledge and information but high on passion and enthusiasm.

There is another world — just as real — where many of my brothers and sisters exist in deprivation, struggle for survival, and experience great need. This is the suffering world. Spiritual emptiness, corrupt leadership, extreme poverty, pandemic diseases, and crippling illiteracy dominate. In this world, largely unknown to most of us, there are 33 million people infected with HIV, an incurable but preventable viral infection that leads to AIDS when the immune system finally fails. Fifteen million orphans are part of this world — and that number represents just those orphaned as a result of HIV/AIDS; it doesn't include the more than 130 million children orphaned by other diseases or causes. You and I have the opportunity to be Jesus' hands and feet to these brothers and sisters, making him known by our love.

The third world is the unseen spiritual world — *the most real world of all* — in which I am united with God through a personal relationship with his Son, Jesus Christ. This is the world from which I draw the strength, courage, integrity, and love I need in order to live in the other two worlds. If I didn't experience the spiritual world with its eternal perspective, I would burn out from fatigue or emotional overload. God's

Word, quiet times of reflection, worship music that refreshes my soul, and the companionship of other "ruined" friends keep me spiritually healthy. Because of that, I am happy and content to be a citizen of all three worlds. Living with my feet in all three of these worlds is a challenge as I constantly evaluate where to spend my time and energy on a daily basis, but being spiritually grounded makes it all possible.

JOINING THE RANKS
OF THE RUINED

When I speak nowadays to small groups getting ready to go on short-term mission trips, I half jokingly invite them to become members of the Seriously Disturbed, Gloriously Ruined Club. Some of them look at me as though I'm nuts — they can't imagine what I'm talking about, but then they seek me out when they return from their trip and say, "Now I get it; I'm ruined." They are no longer content to live with the focus of their lives being on *their* world — themselves, their problems, their family, their career. Their eyes have been opened to new realities. They have seen how the suffering world lives, and it is now *real.* They cannot ignore the suffering or pretend it doesn't exist. They are compelled to do something about it. They are now willing to live in three worlds, as I do — as seriously disturbed and gloriously ruined people.

What about you? You don't have to go to Africa to prove that you're seriously disturbed and gloriously ruined. That's where dangerous surrender to God led me, but it's not a litmus test of the depth of your obedience to God. What *is* a litmus test of your surrender and obedience to God is how you treat the least among us (see Matthew 25:40). Will you allow God to shake up your comfortable world on behalf of those most in need, whether they live around the world or around the corner? There's got to be somewhere — someplace in your world — where you are demonstrating God's love to the least of these in concrete ways.

In what ways are you allowing God to rearrange your schedule, your finances, your affections, so that you can regularly interact with those he loves? Perhaps you give money to a church or a charitable organization — it's a great beginning step, but it's not enough. Giving financially loosens the grip of materialism and selfishness that we all struggle with, but it can be a way of quieting our conscience while keeping our distance from those in need. Can you point to the sick, the poor, the prisoner, the orphan, the widow, the immigrant you are personally ministering to in Jesus' name? If not, it's time to make some dramatic adjustments in your life.

You won't become ruined by sitting in your living room. You might become disturbed, but you won't be ruined. You can watch a news special on TV, read an article in a magazine, or download a video from the Internet and become disturbed by the suffering in our world. But to become ruined, you'll have to actually *do* something — participate in a rally, volunteer in an after-school program, visit someone in the hospital, attend a conference, read to a blind person, serve a meal at a homeless shelter, travel outside of your own neighborhood, hold an HIV-positive baby, go on a short-term mission trip — *anything* that puts you in direct contact with hurting people. As long as suffering people are a mere statistic to you, you will never become ruined for life as you know it. When suffering becomes personal — with faces and names — and when you hear their stories, you won't be able to remain disconnected.

Cathy Johnson has been gloriously ruined. When others in her small group suggested that they all start volunteering with the homeless community in Orange County, Cathy was completely against it. Her reason? Her brother is homeless, having spurned her attempts to help him, and she was afraid she would run into him. Having a homeless family member is a complex circumstance that she felt no one else in her group could completely understand. To her shock, her group decided to do it anyway. So Cathy cautiously went to a run-down motel that serves the homeless. She served pancakes, talked to the residents, sang some songs, and shared a brief message about the love of Jesus for the residents — and she loved every minute of it! God grabbed Cathy's heart that day — in spite of her fears and serious reservations. She was willing to surrender to God, even to the point of being willing to encounter her brother as she served the homeless. She let God rearrange her values, her attitudes, and even her actions. Today she is the one in the small group always asking, "What's next? What are we going to do in our community for hurting people?" She is ruined — gloriously ruined.

Ruined.

It doesn't sound very attractive. I have cried more tears, felt more pain, and experienced more sorrow than ever before. Hardly a day goes by that my heart doesn't break about something. Sometimes I wonder how many times my heart can break and still survive. I can relate to a woman who attended one of our HIV training events and emailed Elizabeth. The subject line of her email was "Nothing glorious yet about my devastation." She wrote the following:

I responded to Pastor Rick's call to attend the AIDS Summit last year and responded to your invitation to attend the HIV Workshop yesterday. Ever since then, I have been weeping. I have almost forgiven Pastor Rick for encouraging me to attend that summit! You and Kay have mentioned such terms as "seriously disturbed" and "gloriously ruined." My question to you is — what on earth is so "glorious" about this? I am simply "seriously disturbed and utterly devastated."

Yep, she's ruined all right. Me too.

But I'm not just ruined; I'm *gloriously* ruined! I'm more vibrantly alive than I've ever been. I have discovered richness in relationships and work that had eluded me before. I have a better grasp on how to find joy and pleasure in the middle of dire circumstances. Caring for those Jesus loves draws me closer to him. I am certain that my life counts for something significant. I would never go back to who I used to be. Becoming seriously disturbed and gloriously ruined is the best thing that has ever happened to me.

You may find my reaction really strange and hard to understand. You may even be experiencing the same confusion as the woman who wrote the email above — there's nothing glorious yet about being disturbed and ruined. Let me give you some hope! It takes time — weeks, even months — to settle into a new way of viewing the world, of achieving an equilibrium that allows you to feel the pain and sorrow of our world without being overwhelmed by it. Don't short-circuit the process of what God is trying to do in your heart just because it hurts. Give yourself some time to get used to the internal changes he is creating within you.

SURRENDER

Will you let God "ruin" you,
forever altering how you relate to others
in your life and world?

Prayer

Father, I confess that asking you to ruin me is something I'm still considering. I'm not sure I'm ready to ask you to do it. I don't know the implications of such a radical surrender. I *want* to be ready. Will you begin to rearrange me and my way of doing life? I want to create space in my heart for hurting people. Help me to grow every day in my willingness to let you gloriously ruin me.

SAY YES TO GOD

○ Make a list of your hesitations about asking God to ruin you. If you're meeting regularly with a reading partner, be sure to share this list the next time you meet.

○ Ask a few friends to join you in serving someone in need in your community this week.

○ Listen to "I Will Never Be the Same Again" at www .kaywarren.com.

READY, SET, STOP

Taste and see that the LORD is good.
Oh, the joys of those who take refuge in him!
Psalm 34:8 NLT

Faith that is sure of itself is not faith;
faith that is sure of God is the only faith there is.
Oswald Chambers, *My Utmost for His Highest*, December 21

SEPTEMBER 18, 2003 — SIX MONTHS AFTER MY VISITS TO Africa — started like any other day. I was completely unaware that my world was about to come crashing down. It was time for my yearly mammogram — just one of many activities that day to check off my to-do list. The test was simple and uneventful, and afterward I continued with my day's agenda.

The next day, however — a Friday — the doctor's office called and told me I needed to come in for a diagnostic mammogram on Monday. With my heart instantly in my throat, I asked the nurse what was wrong. Of course, she couldn't give me any information — other than just to say there was a need for further tests. I don't know why test results always seem to be delivered on Friday afternoons; it just means you wait anxiously over an entire weekend.

Monday brought a diagnostic mammogram and an ultrasound. The radiologist stared at the film in the darkened room and pointed out areas of calcification, but he assured me it was probably nothing. To be certain, he ordered a needle biopsy for the next day.

My dad's birthday was September 25, and I was planning to fly to Arizona to be with him. Because the radiologist was so casual in my need for a biopsy, I scheduled the test for a time slot right before my flight. Rick wanted to go with me, but I was counting on it being nothing, so I asked my assistant, Marian, to drive me to the appointment at a local hospital.

After my breast was numbed, the radiologist poked and prodded the tissue to get a good sample. A few moments later, he and the nurse assistant were gazing intently at the screen where the biopsy procedure could be observed. He matter-of-factly said, "Yes, I see the lump and the areas of calcification."

I nearly fell off the table. "What lump? What are you talking about? No one said anything to me about a lump!" Without looking at me, he coolly said, "It's almost certainly cancer. We'll know tomorrow for sure." I sank back onto the cold gurney in shock. He and the assistant walked out of the room, leaving me completely alone to absorb the word: *Cancer.*

ROADBLOCK

God had seriously disturbed me. He had dealt a death blow to the Kingdom of Me. I was gloriously ruined for life. I had jumped into my new role as an HIV advocate with great enthusiasm and was having regular discussions with large relief organizations about ways Saddleback Church could partner with their efforts in Africa. I was reading everything I could find about HIV/AIDS and speaking to experts in the field. I'd traveled to Africa twice within six weeks. I attended President Bush's announcement of the President's Emergency Plan for AIDS Relief.

Rick had been with me for part of my second trip to Africa. Under the brilliant African sky one evening, God gave him a vision of how local churches could address the global Goliaths of spiritual emptiness, corrupt leadership, extreme poverty, pandemic disease, and crippling illiteracy. Now, a few months later, our church was on the verge of launching an audacious global strategy called the PEACE Plan to partner with local churches around the world to promote spiritual reconciliation with God, equip servant leaders, assist the poor, care for the sick, and educate the next generation — all in sustainable, reproducible ways. The fledgling HIV/AIDS Initiative at Saddleback was growing. I was ready and poised to serve, passionately energized to end HIV/AIDS in the name of Jesus Christ. Ready, set, go! No — ready, set, stop.

All of my plans and dreams ground to a halt in one moment in time. With the word *cancer* now looming over me, it was a distinct possibility that I was going to become a statistic — one of the 189,500 women in the United States to receive that terrifying diagnosis in 2003.

The first thought that flashed through my brain was "At least it's not HIV; I have a fighting chance with breast cancer." As strange and random as that thought seemed, it showed how my life had already shifted to the world of HIV/AIDS. The next thought brought an instant connection with God.

It was a fragment of a Bible verse: "He knows the way that I take." In my fog of shock and fear, I didn't remember the rest of the verse, who said it, or where it was found in Scripture. All I knew was that although I had been left alone with this potentially life-threatening diagnosis, I wasn't really alone in that strange room. God was with me. He knew the way I was about to take, and he wouldn't leave me to face it by myself.

I managed to get dressed and stumble out of the testing room in a daze. Marian was anxiously waiting for me, and I collapsed into her arms, weeping. She held me, and we cried together for a few minutes, neither of us quite believing that cancer was now a part of my journey. I called Rick from the car, and he was as shocked and incredulous as I was. When we pulled into our driveway, he rushed out to meet me, and again, I was held in the arms of someone who loved me dearly.

That night, I went to my Bible to find the rest of the verse that had given me comfort in the panicked moments following the biopsy. It is so fitting that it is found in Job 23:10 — Job, the archetype of suffering humanity, affirming his faith in the God of the universe and in the goal of his suffering.

> But [God] knows the way that I take;
>   when he has tested me, I will come forth as gold.

I didn't claim an assurance from this verse that if I had cancer I was going to be physically healed, but I did read into it the promise that although the trial might be fiery, "gold" could be produced from the suffering. That was a promise to hang on to through the next five months — a time during which I returned to this verse over and over again.

I had to wait until the next day to get the final word on

the biopsy, so I was on pins and needles. Around noon, the radiologist from the hospital called and began by making a joke. I interrupted his joke and said, "Since you're making a joke, can I assume that I don't have breast cancer?" I couldn't imagine that a professional would keep me in suspense about something so crucial or that he would be so cavalier as to make a joke if I actually had cancer.

He paused and said, "Unfortunately, you *do* have breast cancer." Fighting tears, I gathered a few facts from him — the kind of breast cancer, the size of the tumor, and so on — and then hung up. His bedside manner was nonexistent, and he missed a perfect opportunity to offer comfort to a very scared woman. I often think of him when I speak with sick people; his poor approach reminds me of how tender and gentle I need to be.

Telling our children, my parents, and our closest friends was so hard. But I remember being in a protective cocoon — almost as though I was floating above the situation. While everyone else was afraid and tearful, I was able to be cool and calm, offering reassurance to everyone that it was going to be OK. My feelings had disappeared. Within a week, I had lined up an appointment with an oncologist, who recommended further testing. Those tests determined that surgery was required, and the date was selected. With each visit to the doctor, the news became more unsettling. Not only would I need surgery; I would also have to undergo radiation and probably chemotherapy.

THE CRUCIBLE OF CANCER

One day while getting dressed, I looked in the mirror and thought, "I look the same. How can there be an alien living inside of me trying to kill me?" Suddenly I was overwhelmed with fear, panic, and anger. I ran into my closet and slammed the door. "I don't want to be on this road, God! I want to be on *that* road, the one I *was* on. This is a detour. I don't want this cancer. Take it back! I want the life I was living. Give it back to me now!"

But God didn't do that. He didn't give me back the life I had been living. He didn't take the cancer away. Instead, he allowed surgery, ninety days of chemotherapy, and thirty-five days of radiation. He allowed me to lose my hair and my fingernails. He allowed surgery that left a misshapen body, scars from the sentinel node biopsy, scars from the Port-a-Cath that had to be surgically implanted when the chemotherapy started to corrode the veins in my arm, and permanent tattoos on my chest that marked the radiation field. He allowed me to experience hospitalization after three of the four chemo treatments because of severe reactions. He allowed the chemotherapy to rob my short-term memory, perhaps forever, and to leave my brain feeling addled and dull. He allowed what seems to be permanent nerve impairment in all of the pressure points on my body, making sleeping or staying in one position for a long time sometimes unbearable. He allowed me to feel the sting of being ignored by some people whom I had assumed would be there for me. My faith was being tested in the crucible of cancer.

I was unpleasantly surprised at my own reaction to God after a couple of months of treatment woes. One day, sitting on the couch with my friend Elizabeth, I began to explore my thought and feelings. "This is embarrassing for me to admit," I told her, "but I just don't *get* God at all! His ways are a complete mystery to me. My suffering is awful — but mine is just a microcosm of what billions are enduring at this very moment. Do you have any idea how intense the suffering is for billions of people *right now?*"

But I had so many advantages. Even though I had breast cancer and wasn't tolerating the treatment very well, I had everything I needed — the love and support of my family and friends, access to excellent medical treatment, a home with a comfy bed to sink into when I felt sick, and food (when I could actually eat). I had it easy in comparison to those for whom their entire existence, from birth until death, would be about survival and suffering. Easy in comparison to the women who were sold into prostitution by husbands, parents, or neighbors. Easy in comparison to those with AIDS who had no medication. Easy in comparison to the men who work from dawn to dusk in backbreaking labor to provide for their families. Easy in comparison to those unjustly rotting in prisons around the world. From a larger perspective, my suffering was so small.

My voice shook with frustration as I asked Elizabeth, "Why would God create a world in which such dreadful suffering can exist?"

STORMING HEAVEN'S DOORS

There is a tendency in all of us to shake our fists at God in anger and recrimination when life smacks us around. Frequently, our response is to pull away from him in disappointment, disillusionment, and bitterness. We instinctively know that he could prevent or at least mitigate whatever suffering comes into our lives; ultimately he is in charge of our universe.

"It's all his fault," we reason.

I was like Job that day, wearily storming heaven's doors, insisting on answers to my questions, my doubts, my fears, my anger. I knew the theological truths about heaven and the ways in which this life prepares us for the next, but my conclusion was "The system sucks. There has to be a better way. I don't get it at all." I rested on my couch — a pale, bald creature physically weakened from chemotherapy and nauseated; emotionally drained by fear, anxiety, and depression; and spiritually aching, bombarded with existential questions of cosmic proportions.

"I need to hear from God!" I moaned. "I need satisfactory answers that will ease the pain of my suffering. I can barely stand my own pain, but I'm also feeling the pain of people I don't even know. What is God's explanation for this broken system?"

My passionate yet weak voice trailed away into silence. Elizabeth wisely didn't try to shut me up, placate me with the standard answers, or tell me that I was playing with fire. She cried with me, held my hand, and confirmed that my pain was real. She assured me that my questions were valid and affirmed that I was doing the right thing — running *to* God in my pain, not *away* from him. Gently she spoke the conviction of her heart: "He is good; whether or not you and I can see it, he is good."

My agonized soul did not get an audience with God that day — at least not in the way I was asking for. But through the compassionate voice of a friend, God spoke to me and reminded me of who he is, of his unchanging character, and of his promise to never leave me.

Suffering permitted the trappings of normal life to be stripped away, exposing my faith to reality testing. It allowed me to discover the holes, inconsistencies, and weak spots in my relationship to God that I wasn't aware of. Suddenly I was faced with this challenge: I claim to love and trust God, but do I really? I *say* that I believe he is a loving Father, but do I really believe it? How quickly do I turn on him? How fast do I jettison my beliefs when my life and my beliefs collide? How viciously do I accuse him when pain, sorrow, disappointment, betrayal, tragedy, or losses come my way? Will my faith survive the tests? Do I even have faith?

The Bible says that troubles and trials put our faith on display so our true colors are seen. It doesn't matter what we *say* we believe; a watching world evaluates whether or not our faith is real by our reactions to suffering:

> Consider it a sheer gift, friends, when tests and challenges come at you from all sides. You know that under pressure, your faith-life is forced into the open and shows its true colors. So don't try to get out of anything prematurely. Let it do its work so you become mature and well-developed, not deficient in any way.
>
> *James 1:2–4 MSG*

Searing heat and gale-force winds come into every life. No one is immune or exempt. Sometimes we see it coming—a siren blows, and we're alerted that something bad is headed our way. Other times there is no warning—unexpectedly our feet get knocked out from under us, and we're on the ground before we know what hit us. In those times, our faith-life is exposed, and we have to ask ourselves, "What am I holding on to?"

I'm not a sailor, but I love the imagery in the 2003 movie *Master and Commander*. During a fierce storm, Captain Jack Aubrey (played by Russell Crowe) strapped himself to the mast of his ship so he wouldn't be washed overboard by the enormous waves. The ship pitched one direction and then the other, and although the colossal waves tore at his body, he remained safely tethered to the mast.

Years before I had cancer, I made a commitment to God and said, "I am yours to do with as you wish. I know I won't understand you fully, and I will probably keep asking questions, but I know you love me." I lashed myself to the mast, so that no matter how strong the winds may blow, how violently the sea crashes over my little ship, or how powerfully the storm threatens to rip me from the mast, I will not be moved. The "mast" of my faith is this bedrock truth: *God is good.*

Because I am completely confident that God's character is unimpeachable — pure, spotless, wholesome, wholly righteous, with not even a hint of evil — he can be trusted with all that concerns me. The Bible speaks with one voice throughout its pages, revealing a God who is good to the core. The psalmist declares, "Good and upright is the LORD" (Psalm 25:8). A choir of priests sing, "He is good; his love endures forever" (2 Chronicles 5:13). Jesus says of his Father, "No one is good — except God alone" (Mark 10:18).

Being convinced of that truth, I run *to* him in my pain, not *away from* him. I'm certain that God uses suffering to test me, to purify me, and to make me stronger, and because of that, I'm willing to stay connected to him. I long for my responses to pain to be ones that reveal my trust in him and his goodness. This is how joy and sorrow coexist. The apostle Peter gives wise counsel about this subject:

> So be truly glad. There is wonderful joy ahead, even though you have to endure many trials for a little while. These trials will show that your faith is genuine. It is being tested as fire tests and purifies gold — though your faith is far more precious than mere gold. So when your faith remains strong through many trials, it will bring you much praise and glory and honor on the day when Jesus Christ is revealed to the whole world.
>
> *1 Peter 1:6 – 7 NLT*

All cancer is not the same, and breast cancer is one in which the doctors will never pronounce you cured. They will tell you that you're in remission, which means they can't find any cancer in your body, but there is always the possibility that some rogue cells escaped the surgery, radiation, and chemotherapy and are floating through your system, only to resurface at a later date. That possibility began to fill my thoughts as I approached the end of treatment and the fear level began to rise again. The what-ifs began to consume me.

The passage in Job that had brought wonderful comfort in the beginning now became my lifeline. I found peace in knowing that while I cannot control *how long* I live, I can control *how* I live. One of my mottoes is "Control the controllables and leave the uncontrollables to God." I don't get to determine the length of my days, but I can determine the *quality* of the days given to me. I wanted "gold" — character — to be produced from my fiery suffering.

I have determined to live my life, not looking over my shoulder to see if cancer is catching up with me, but looking forward to each day I receive. At the same time, all of my illusions about any guarantees of long life are gone and there is a sense of urgency about what I do. I am keenly aware of how fragile life is, how brief and how holy it is. Knowing life's fragility causes me to be more intentional, more passionate, more convinced of the sweetness of this moment, and more convicted than ever that I am here for a reason. I don't want to waste a second of the time I have been given.

But I wasn't through with cancer.

A year and a half after finishing treatment for breast cancer, I had a suspicious mole removed. I got the results while we were on a family vacation in another state. The doctor said, "Unfortunately, Mrs. Warren, it's melanoma. It looks like it hasn't spread very far into the dermis, but you will need to have a wide excision surgery to remove all of the surrounding tissue." For the second time in two years, I was listening to a physician tell me that I had cancer. He proceeded to go over the statistical probability of my being alive and cancer free in ten years. "This just can't be happening," I thought. "Cancer *again*?" My stomach churned, my heart beat faster, and images of nausea, vomiting, baldness, and fatigue flashed before me. "God, I can't go through that another time. Please don't make me!" Once the phone call was over, my children and Rick gathered around me once again and prayed for me.

I came home from our vacation to face another surgery. We waited anxiously for the pathology report to learn if the melanoma had spread. To our enormous relief, it hadn't. This time, instead of losing a breast, I ended up with a four-inch scar on my shoulder and a doctor's appointment every three months for the next few years. Having cancer a second time simply reinforced my determination to live my life very intentionally with no wasted moments. It was another clarion call to fulfill God's purposes with the time I am given.

FROM SYMPATHY TO EMPATHY

My first international trip posttreatment for breast cancer was to Thailand and Cambodia in the summer of 2004. I was frail from the toxic chemicals and radiation. My hair had begun to grow back, but it was so curly and uneven that I looked like a poodle with a short mullet. I had worn a wig since losing my hair six months before but decided to leave it at home so I wouldn't have to deal with it in the summer heat of Southeast Asia. People stared; I was conscious of how strange I looked, especially in a place where many women have long, lustrous hair.

In Cambodia, we were taken to a house made of reeds and bamboo to visit a woman dying of AIDS. Sitting on her raised bed, she was surrounded by women in her church who were taking care of her; they sat shoulder to shoulder on her bed. Through an interpreter, she hesitantly spoke of how her husband had infected her and then died. She spoke of the various setbacks she had encountered with AIDS, including one medication that had caused her to lose her hair. She looked into the faces of each woman seated near her and related how each one had done something special for her. One of the women had donated blood to help treat her friend's anemia. Others took her to the hospital. Another brought food and cared for her children. It was clear that these women — sisters in her suffering — were pillars of strength for her in her pain. She spoke of the nearness of God and how she couldn't imagine going through this awful time without him.

I stood in the swelteringly hot little bamboo house with Elizabeth and had an epiphany. The Cambodian woman's pain was not a mystery to me; her suffering was not theoretical. I, too, had received a life-threatening diagnosis, and if I had not had access to miraculous medication, the cancer would have eventually killed me. I had taken a medication so powerful it made my hair fall out. The "cure" had made me nauseated and weak. But just as with this Cambodian woman, my relationships spelled the difference between hope and despair. I too had a relationship with God, who had been near me. I too had a family and a small group who gave and gave of themselves to me. It was a different illness, and I was halfway around the world; but I could identify with a fellow sufferer in a whole new way.

I got it.

Not only did cancer teach me about suffering in general; suffering also became personal. I could empathize now — and not just with the negative aspects of suffering, such as the fear of dying, treatments that made me violently ill, scars that will never go away, and depression that settled like a blanket over my emotions. I could also identify with the blessings hidden in the messiness of suffering — the "gold" it produced. I now knew God was the only one who could be counted on completely. I learned that although there is much about him I don't understand, he is completely trustworthy. I discovered that he gave me loved ones to help carry the burden. I figured out that life's brevity and fragility make it precious and worth living to the fullest extent of my passions and his purposes. These are lessons you only learn through pain — the kind of lessons Paul encourages the Corinthians to learn:

> All praise to God, the Father of our Lord Jesus Christ. God is our merciful Father and the source of all comfort. He comforts us in all our troubles so that we can comfort others. When they are troubled, we will be able to give them the same comfort God has given us. For the more we suffer for Christ, the more God will shower us with his comfort through Christ. Even when we are weighed down with troubles, it is for your comfort and salvation! For when we ourselves are comforted, we will certainly comfort you. Then you can patiently endure the same things we suffer. We are confident that as you share in our sufferings, you will also share in the comfort God gives us.
>
> *2 Corinthians 1:3 – 7 NLT*

RUNNING TO GOD
IN TIMES OF TROUBLE

In every crisis — a cancer diagnosis, the loss of a job, a divorce, a child who rejects your values, the ending of a friendship — we have the opportunity to run toward God in our pain, or we can choose to run from him. Running *to* God in our suffering rather than *from* him allows us to experience this deep comfort for ourselves. Running toward him doesn't make the pain go away or make an impossible situation suddenly neat and tidy, but it does give our pain meaning.

The meaning in our suffering isn't always immediately apparent. It may be months, years, or even decades before you catch a glimpse of how God used the sorrow or suffering to accomplish his purposes. But bringing good out of evil is what he does best, and I see this clearly in the life of my friend Dr. Susan Hillis.

Susan was a busy woman — an epidemiologist with the Centers for Disease Control in Atlanta, Georgia, and the mother of three young children — Cristi, age eleven; Jonny, age nine; and Trevor, age two. On the day before Jonny's tenth birthday, Susan and her husband and children were out on a bike ride. Jonny was hit by a car and died at the accident scene. Susan and her husband, Brian, were completely devastated by the loss. The next day, Cristi said to Susan, "Mom, we need to adopt a child."

Susan and Brian were crushed by grief and couldn't fathom why Cristi would be pushing for them to adopt a child when they hadn't even buried Jonny. Susan tried to brush aside Cristi's remarks, but Cristi was insistent: "Mom, I think God wants us to adopt a child. I think you should pray about it." Within a year, Susan and her husband began to sense that Cristi might be right. They felt that God had filled their hearts with an enormous capacity to love children — especially children who had also suffered the loss of family members. Tiny glimmers of meaning in Jonny's death were beginning to surface for them.

They inquired about adopting an orphan from Latin America, since Susan and Brian speak fluent Spanish, but those doors closed. Another adoption agency sent them a video of two Russian children, Anya, age eight, and Alyosha, age seven. They were convinced that these two children were the ones God wanted to join the Hillis family. Over the next six years, Susan and Brian adopted not only Anya and Alyosha but six other Russian orphans as well, who now live in the safety, protection, and love of their family. Yes, you're counting correctly — Susan and Brian have ten children.

Most of us would have understood if Susan and her husband had closed their hearts to children in the bleak sadness of losing Jonny. The pain of seeing other kids his age would just pour salt in their wounds, we reason. But they courageously surrendered their lives, their children, and their future to God. They didn't run *from* him but *to* him in their pain. By opening their hearts and homes to children stripped of family — just as they had been stripped of family — they allowed God to redeem what felt like a meaningless tragedy. Susan and Brian's suffering produced "gold" in their lives. Something of incredible value has been produced in the fire of their sorrow — something that wouldn't have been produced any other way.

All of us hate sorrow. We hate the suffering that comes from living in a broken world, the difficulties that bring us to our knees, the tears that roll down our cheeks like a flood. But in ways that can happen only in God's design, transformation gradually emerges from the ashes of the fire. Men who formerly lived selfishly for themselves find satisfaction in serving others. Women who used to need everything to be perfect before they could be happy find that it takes much less to bring a smile to their faces. Those with control issues find that surrender brings peace. Those so sure of themselves and their rightness find themselves gentler — softer, more flexible and pliable. They become more like Jesus.

François Fénelon was no stranger to suffering, having

endured years of gossip, persecution, and even banishment for his faith. Through it all, he never doubted that God used his suffering to make him more like Jesus:

> I am awed by what suffering can produce. You and I are nothing without the cross. I agonize and cry when the cross is working within me, but when it is over I look back in admiration for what God has accomplished. Of course I am then ashamed that I bore it so poorly. I have learned so much from my foolish reactions.[9]

Two bouts of cancer threatened to dismantle the dreams I had for my life — dreams I believed God had inspired. These health scares, awful as they were, forced me to examine what I believed about God and his character and helped me settle once and for all on the side of a faith that cannot be shaken by circumstances. Many days I felt as though I was flying blind — unable to see God with my eyes but knowing for certain that he was in control and that he was *good*.

Your life may seem charmed. Cancer may never darken your doorway, never haunt your health. You may never live through a tragedy that threatens to devastate you or those you love. But somewhere along the way, the dreams you have for your life will be threatened by *something*. Your faith in the goodness of God *will* be tested. What will you do when it seems as though all that is good in your life has turned to ashes? At some point you will be tempted to declare that you've had enough and to walk away from God. When it seems as though he has set you up for something wonderful, only to yank it away — ready, set, stop — how will you respond? Remember: our faith-life shows its true colors when you are put to the test. Learning through your own suffering that God is good and that he can be trusted will prepare you to face the suffering and evil you encounter in the lives of others.

SURRENDER

Will you surrender your demand for God to order your life the way you want it to be ordered?

Heavenly Father, I confess that I'm inclined to run away from you when trouble comes my way. I get angry and frustrated because of the circumstances of my life and start to wonder if you really are a good God. Forgive me for demanding that my life hold no pain or hardship. In this moment of quiet reflection, I choose to bring my broken heart, broken spirit, and broken body to you — I come running to you. Would you please comfort me? I don't want to waste my suffering anymore. Please use the fires of difficult times to produce "gold" in my life so that the things that cloud the purity of my love for you will be burned away. Today help me to live out what I say I believe.

SAY YES TO GOD

○ Think about a time when you experienced a "ready, set, stop" moment in your journey. Write a few sentences that describe how you reacted. If you meet with a reading partner, share your reflections the next time you talk.

○ Memorize Psalm 118:1: "Give thanks to the LORD, for he is good; his love endures forever."

○ Listen to Kay's message "The Spiritual Side of Breast Cancer" at www.kaywarren.com.

EXPOSING EVIL

Who will help me fight against the wicked?
Who will stand with me against those who do evil?
Psalm 94:16 NCV

Perhaps the greatest challenge in
confronting evil is simply getting started.
Gary Haugen, *Terrify No More*

THE STREET OF THE LITTLE FLOWERS WAS BARELY WIDE
enough for the car to pass through. On one side were tiny
sidewalk cafés where Western men sat drinking beer with
petite, middle-aged Cambodian women. They eyed the car
with suspicion, pausing in their conversations to see who
might be driving in this part of town. Across the narrow
street were ramshackle buildings with metal doors padlocked shut. My skin crawled with horror to know that on
the other side of those padlocked doors were little girls —
some of them as young as five or six — who would be offered
as sexual partners to the men sitting in the cafés as soon as
it was dusk. We were told that the younger the child, the
more money she was worth — virgins are highly prized in
the world of sexual perversion. For a mere $300, a man could
"buy" one of these little ones, take her to a hotel for up to a

week, use her in any way he chose, and then return her to the brothel where he had found her.

Evil, unspeakable evil.

His face contorted with pain, soft words emerging from a throat nearly closed with the effort of holding back the tears, Bishop John spoke of his dear young niece. Sometime during the one hundred days of genocide in 1994 when Rwanda shuddered, convulsed, and imploded on itself, she was raped and beaten. Not satisfied with the harm they had already inflicted, her tormentors painstakingly peeled back the skin on her arms to her elbows to reveal muscles and ligaments. There was more. Hatred fueled the fire burning deep in the hearts of those who tortured her; they muted her dying screams by cutting off her head.

Evil, unspeakable evil.

In Tuol Sleng, a crumbling former school building in Phnom Penh, Cambodia, I walked from interrogation room to interrogation room, prison cell to prison cell, ending up in a room where white skulls were precisely stacked behind a glass case. Black-and-white photographs of the faces of men, women, and children who were tortured and then murdered lined the walls. Their captors found a macabre pleasure in recording the likenesses of their victims before they butchered them. Large murals now etched in my memory depicted horrible ways of killing. One scene was of a mother lying on the ground, straining to grab her baby away from a gleeful soldier. He was swinging the infant toward a tree trunk in the same way a batter swings at a baseball. Video reenactments of the brutality were available for viewing. Museum docents told of the mass indoctrination of children and youth to become betrayers of parents, aunts, uncles, siblings, neighbors — twisting the love and loyalty toward family into love and loyalty to a brutal regime instead. Millions slaughtered — and a country left bruised and battered, forever branded with the legacy of genocide.

Evil, unspeakable evil.

One lovely spring morning in 2007, a mentally ill gunman began to unleash his rage, his frustration, and his hatred on unsuspecting classmates at Virginia Tech University. With no visible emotion, he calmly and methodically entered classrooms, filling the bodies of strangers and acquaintances with bullets, shooting many more times than was necessary to kill them. Within minutes, at least fifteen people were wounded, and thirty-three others (twenty-seven students and five professors, plus the gunman) were horribly, inexplicably dead.

Evil, unspeakable evil.

I can barely breathe as I type these words. My chest is gripped as if with a vise, and I keep expelling big sighs as I attempt to put words on the paper through my tears. I shake my head hard, as if shaking my head will fling the sickening images away. How I wish these stories were fictional or exaggerated to illustrate a point. How I wish these examples of evil were isolated incidents — anomalies in an otherwise idyllic world where goodness, kindness, and brotherly love reign supreme. How I wish I could just change the channel and make it all go away — the way I do when I see on my TV screen the upsetting images of children with bloated bellies.

But evil is real, and evil must be exposed, opposed, and stopped.

God desires to not only disturb us by the suffering we see but also to seriously disturb us by opening our eyes to the evil that is behind suffering. You might be tempted to skip this chapter and move on to the more positive, uplifting sections of the book. I understand the urge to escape the unsettling and upsetting stories I've told. Denial is a God-given psychological response that protects us when reality becomes more than we can bear, but denial is only meant to be short-lived; it is not intended to become a habit, a way of life. Sadly, for many of us, denying the reality, pervasiveness, and enormity of evil is standard operating procedure.

Those of us who live in resource-rich countries have the luxury of pretending that life is pretty good for everyone. Sure, we've all got problems and challenges, but few of us come face-to-face with stark evil on a daily basis. Perhaps those in law enforcement, social services, and the prison system see the ugly underbelly of humanity as part of their daily routine, but the rest of us blithely live our lives ignorant and unaware of the way unopposed evil savages our planet every day. When we do bump up against evil, we're unprepared — shocked, in fact, and aghast that this terrible thing has invaded our lives, as though we shouldn't *have* to deal with it.

I, too, responded with shock, but I shouldn't have been so surprised when I first saw the evil I described for you. The Bible pulls no punches when it refers to the evil lurking in broken humanity. It describes the depravity we inherited from Adam and Eve in vivid and depressing detail:

> The LORD observed the extent of human wickedness on the earth, and he saw that everything they thought or imagined was consistently and totally evil.
>
> *Genesis 6:5 NLT*

Fools say in their hearts,
  "There is no God."
They are corrupt, their deeds are vile;
  there is no one who does good.
The LORD looks down from heaven
  on the human race
to see if there are any who understand,
  any who seek God.
All have turned away, all have become corrupt;
  there is no one who does good,
  not even one.

Psalm 14:1 – 3 TNIV

This is the evil in everything that happens under the sun: The same destiny overtakes all. The hearts of men, moreover, are full of evil and there is madness in their hearts while they live, and afterward they join the dead.

Ecclesiastes 9:3

The heart is deceitful above all things
  and beyond cure.
Who can understand it?

Jeremiah 17:9

For the six of us in the van driving through the Street of the Little Flowers in Cambodia, the reality of evil abruptly flooded our senses. Elizabeth, her son Peter, my son Matthew, and a young couple from Saddleback had accompanied me to Thailand and Cambodia. Now we were filled with a mixture of shock, nausea, and rage. Who would intentionally do such appalling things to little girls? What kind of men and women peddled the bodies of children who were being held against their will? What drives men to travel thousands of miles to indulge their lusts at the expense of a child's innocence and health? In my outrage, my thoughts were murderous; I wanted to *hurt* the men who were waiting like vultures. I wanted to castrate them in violent ways, to make them suffer for the suffering they were causing. At the same time, I wished I could be a comic book heroine who would knock down the padlocked doors, swoop in, and release the thousands of captive children and then deposit them into loving homes.

What could I do against such despicable evil? I was just an ordinary woman.

If Bishop John had a hard time recounting his niece's death, part of me wanted to stuff my fingers in my ears and loudly mutter, "Lalalalalala — I can't hear you!" Bishop John's niece was one of a million others murdered in the Rwanda genocide. The brutality of her death was not much different from that of the deaths of her neighbors, her friends, her schoolmates. Rwanda is filled with genocide sites — many of them churches where the hunted ran for sanctuary, only to discover that their "protectors" were their betrayers. Blood still stains the brick walls. Mass graves are cemented over, but mummified bodies are still being discovered in latrines, wells, and other hiding places. No one was left unscathed by the evil that crushed the beautiful Land of a Thousand Hills.

The exposure to evil at Tuol Sleng created even more feelings of helplessness and powerlessness against an evil almost too great to comprehend. Sickened, shocked, horrified, and filled with leaden sadness, those in our group found ourselves incapable of conversation as we drove back to our hotel. What can you say when you've just witnessed the wickedness that infiltrates the hearts of fellow human beings? How do you even form words graphic enough to convey what you saw? I walked like a robot into my room, not really seeing anyone or anything. My mind replayed the atrocities of that prison, going over and over the bleak cells, the tools of torture, the skulls, the doomed faces in the photographs. In my head I could hear the screams, the wailing, and the unheeded pleas for mercy. All I wanted was to escape from this place where raw evil had happened.

After a while, evil numbs. Minds and hearts, capable of absorbing only so much, shut down.

CHANGING THE CHANNEL

What does God want us to do about evil? Is there really anything one person can do? I can tell you what he *doesn't* want us to do — ignore it, deny it, pretend it doesn't exist, close our hearts and minds to it, or hope it goes away by itself. He doesn't want us to appease it, placate it, compromise with it, coexist with it, justify it, excuse it, or call it by another name. In God's value system, these responses are as wicked as endorsing, cooperating with, or embracing evil.

Evil will not go away by itself. It only grows more insidious by the day. It encroaches on the good, with only one goal in mind: domination and elimination of the good.

We live at a time in history in which the concept of good and evil is sometimes mocked, ridiculed, condescended to, or completely ignored. To frame the world in such terms can get you labeled as sensational or moralistic. To believe there is a cosmic struggle going on between good and evil is laughable in some circles and often easily dismissed with a wave of the hand and a condescending smile. But I find it impossible to converse about evil and the accompanying darkness without using terms such as *fight, battle, war, weapons,* and *victory.* To do so makes some people uncomfortable. I don't know how else to talk about it; if you don't believe it's a battle, pick up your newspaper tonight and skim the headlines (better yet, read all the gory details).

You might be a bit puzzled at this discussion of evil in the middle of a book on surrender. Perhaps you're asking, "What does evil have to do with my personal surrender to God's call on my life?" As you'll see, acknowledging the reality of evil and then accepting God's command to expose it and oppose it are integral parts of being courageously surrendered.

The most common reaction to evil in our world is to deny it exists, to believe it's just your imagination. In fact, one increasingly popular school of thought — Scientology — believes that trillions of years ago there were aliens who came to earth and left their dead spirits here. Those dead spirits implanted something in our minds called engrams, which make us *think* there is such a thing as evil, but there really isn't. It's just in our minds.

Another common point of view is to blame evil on no one in particular, but to chalk up all the tragedies, immense suffering, and injustice to karma — an invisible principle that goes into effect based on our choices. Karma is a response to my mistakes, bad decisions, and actions in a previous life; if I messed up in a past life, then I will reap the consequences in this current life. This perspective has practical implications. Rather than trying to eliminate or fight evil, we should just make better choices *now* so that the next life will be better. Why have compassion on a suffering person if you believe they brought suffering on themselves?

The Bible teaches us that evil is real—and so is the person behind it all. I love the original Star Wars trilogy and have watched it a dozen times with my son Matthew. But evil is not the dark side of an energy force that consists of both good and bad. Evil is not an impersonal power that floats through the universe. Evil comes from a rebellious being who tried to take over God's rightful place; the Bible calls him Satan, or the Evil One. When God threw him out of heaven, Satan took a third of heaven's angels with him to wreak havoc in our world. Together they have invaded earth and are on a mission to trash everything in sight, having adopted a very real "take no prisoners" approach. The Bible portrays our fight against evil as a cosmic spiritual battle: "This is not a wrestling match against a human opponent. We are wrestling with rulers, authorities, the powers who govern this world of darkness, and spiritual forces that control evil in the heavenly world" (Ephesians 6:12 GWT).

Evil is very personal—it's nasty, vicious, gross, and disgusting; it's unbelievably cruel; it's heartbreaking, mind-blowing, and soul shattering. It's *real*, and it must be acknowledged and dealt with—not just by a few but by all.

Perhaps you've been choosing to deal with it the way I did for most of my life—change the channel. Don't like what you see on a particular TV station? Click—change the channel. Find the news too depressing? Click. Think that war and death and casualties are too upsetting? Click. Can't bear to see one more starving skeletal child? Click. Another ad for a relief agency? Click. Ah, now here's one I like—how the Hollywood rich and famous spend their money on baubles, bangles, boats, and binges. Or maybe this one is even better—a reality show! Which narcissistic singer-to-be will get humiliated on tonight's show? Or my personal favorite: Which Orange County housewife can out-spend, out-drink, out-party, out-decorate, out – plastic surgery her neighbor? Now we're talking *quality* entertainment!

Reality? Hardly.

Could it be that we have substituted fake "reality" so that we don't have to think too much about *real* reality? Don't get me wrong — I like TV as much as the next person, but something warped is happening to us.

I wonder if we try to ignore evil because we don't want to feel the pain. We tell ourselves that we have enough trouble, enough challenges, enough struggles of our own. "I've got so much on my own plate; how can I possibly feel the pain others are feeling?"

Avoidance of pain isn't the only reason we turn our eyes away from the evil in this world. I recognize from my own past behavior that by ignoring evil's pain on the faces around me, I believed I didn't have to accept responsibility for doing anything about it. How many times have you passed a homeless man or woman holding a "Will Work for Food" or "Homeless Veteran" sign with your eyes averted? As long as you don't make eye contact, it's fairly easy to drive past him with no twinges of guilt. But if you make eye contact, suddenly you are confronted with the truth that this is a *fellow human being* with a name, a face, and a story. Something tugs at your heart and you start to think, "I have to do something about this." But just as quickly as that faint thought of personal responsibility tickles the edges of your consciousness, other thoughts rush in and crowd out the tenderness: "I don't have time to get involved. Besides, he is probably a slacker or a drunk or an addict. It's his own fault he has to beg for food!"

We choose apathy.

Jake Thoene writes, "Apathy and evil. The two work hand in hand. They are the same, really.... Evil wills it; apathy allows it. Evil hates the innocent and the defenseless most of all. Apathy doesn't care as long as it's not personally inconvenienced."[10]

The Bible tells us this is not the appropriate response to brokenness and evil: "Anyone who knows the right thing to do, but does not do it, is sinning" (James 4:17 NCV). You know there's evil in the world; I do too. If we know it, and choose to do nothing about it, the Bible says we're sinning.

The biblical principle of confronting evil is part of the mandate from our justice-loving God. Dr. Martin Luther King Jr. affirmed this principle when he declared, "He who passively accepts evil is as much involved in it as he who helps to perpetrate it."[11]

Do you get that? Dr. King says that anyone who accepts evil without standing up against it is actually cooperating with it. This was true for the Christians and anyone else who ignored the fight for civil rights for African Americans in the 1950s and '60s, and it applies today. If Christ-followers do not speak up and take action against injustice and evil — abortion, child abuse, domestic violence, exploitation and neglect of orphaned children, human slavery, and so forth — we are as liable as those who instigate it. We let it happen. We are guilty.

Tough to hear.

There is a sobering incident in the Old Testament that illustrates how God feels about ignoring evil. The children of Israel, God's chosen people, were supposed to follow him alone. Every once in while, they would get off track and follow the false gods of the pagan nations around them. Several times in their history, they worshiped the Ammonite god Molech, who was the god of fire. In the worship ceremonies of the Ammonites, young children were burned alive as a sacrifice to Molech. God sternly warns the Israelites: "If the people of the land look the other way as if nothing had happened when that man gives his child to the god Molech . . . , I will resolutely reject . . . all who join him" (Leviticus 20:4 – 5 MSG).

In the same way, evil permeates our world 24/7. There's not a second of the day that evil is not happening in the most profound, perverse, gross, and painful manner — and with instant global information sharing, we are made aware of it in unparalleled ways. While this doesn't mean that the weight of closing down evil on a global scale rests entirely on my frail shoulders, I believe I am responsible to do what I can where I live. I can't single-handedly tackle evil around the world, but I can make a concrete difference in the lives of people who are in my community. I can't find a home for the world's 143 million orphans, but I can care for the orphans and vulnerable children in Orange County in a variety of meaningful ways (go to www.orphansandthechurch.com for more information on what you and your church can do). I can't end hunger and poverty for the half of the world who live on less than one dollar a day, but I can feed a homeless person in my community. I can't make living conditions better for every prisoner around the globe, but I can visit prisoners in the jail in my city. I can't make HIV/AIDS go away for the 33 million people infected, but I can march in the local AIDS Walk to show that I care about people who are HIV positive. Unless we stop ignoring and denying the evil that we can see, hear, taste, feel, and smell in our own communities, God will hold us accountable for looking the other way as if nothing is going on. We *must* face evil squarely, get in tune with the damage it causes, and, most of all, allow ourselves to *feel* the pain evil inflicts, or it will settle even more deeply into the dark corners of our cities, our institutions, our culture, and ultimately our very lives.

I cannot ignore it anymore. I cannot just take up space on this planet, blissfully living my comfortable life as I ignore evil and the way it debauches and destroys life. I cannot pretend that little girls are not being sold *today* to men who will hurt their fragile bodies and tender psyches. I cannot pretend that millions are not living in squalor, hoping to survive one more day in refugee camps. I cannot pretend that women are not raped and brutalized every single day. I cannot pretend that men and women are not kidnapped, stripped of their dignity, forced to do humiliating things for the pleasure of their captors, viciously tortured and murdered for their beliefs. I cannot pretend that millions are not kicked off land they own, cheated out of their rights, their belongings, or the money due them. Truly, the list is endless were we to try to catalog the evils done 24/7, every single day of every year.

I'm done changing the channel.

Dangerous surrender calls you to be done with it too. God clearly calls us to oppose evil in every form — to bring it to the light of day and then get rid of it. Here's how the Bible describes this reality and our responsibility:

SAY YES TO GOD

Take no part in the worthless deeds of evil and darkness; instead, expose them.... But their evil intentions
will be exposed when the light shines on them, for the
light makes everything visible.

Ephesians 5:11, 13 – 14 NLT

If you move a big rock, it's not unusual to find weird, ugly
bugs living underneath it. When exposed to the bright light
of the sun, they will scatter and run for cover under some
other rock. That's what we're supposed to be doing in our
world — exposing the deeds of darkness to the light of God's
justice and holiness. Yes, some of the evildoers will avoid
getting caught; they will just grow craftier in hiding and disguising their deeds. But we are to do all that we can to push
back the darkness wherever we find it.

PUSHING BACK THE DARKNESS

Not only are we to stop ignoring evil and start exposing it;
the Bible says we are to learn how to hate evil: "Let those
who love the LORD hate evil" (Psalm 97:10).

As a Christ-follower, it might surprise you to learn that
God instructs us to hate anything, but he makes it clear that
evil is something we are to hate. We are to become broken-
hearted, disturbed, and outraged by it.

There are at least three weapons you can use in your efforts
to refuse to accept evil and to learn to hate it: stop laughing at
it, stop compromising with it, and start resisting it.

Beware of evil disguised as humor. No one intends to
accept evil into their lives; it creeps in over time when we let
down our guard. The slippery slope of accepting evil often

begins with laughing at things that once were considered immoral or perverse. When you start to laugh at it, you start to accept it. How many times have you seen this happen on television? Moving the moral compass downward begins not with the dramatic series but with the comedies.

A second way to learn to hate evil is to stop compromising with it. We have become so fearful of being labeled intolerant that we have begun to call evil good. Once you go down that road, you lose the critical ability to distinguish between good and evil anymore: "If the godly give in to the wicked, it's like polluting a fountain or muddying a spring" (Proverbs 25:26 NLT).

Why is compromise with evil so dangerous? The Bible tells us that compromise with evil eventually leads us to participate in it: "You must not follow the crowd in doing wrong" (Exodus 23:2 NLT).

When I was in high school, I had a close friend who began to hang around with a rather wild crowd. I asked him why he spent time with these kids who were known for their parties, use of alcohol, and experimentation with sex. He defensively replied, "I'm not doing anything wrong. I'm not participating. I'm just hanging out with them." You probably can guess the end of the story.

I wonder how many of you could give a testimony of what has happened in your life when you were "just hanging out" with certain people. At first, you refrained from doing what they were doing. But it didn't take long before you began to participate; the line between "just looking" and "doing it too" is very thin. The amazing capacity we have for self-deception gets us into trouble over and over again.

But be careful. Don't mishear me. Please don't use the

warning to be cautious about hanging out with a crowd headed in the wrong direction as an excuse for not engaging or getting to know people who are different from you. Don't justify your hard heart by claiming they are "sinners." Jesus made a career out of being with the "wrong" people! Unlike us, he didn't use those relationships as a testing ground to see how close to the edge of sinful behavior he could get without actually sinning; his goal was to demonstrate God's unconditional love and to point them to a more satisfying way of living — one that far surpassed their meager attempts at experiencing the good life.

The progression down the slippery slope of laughter at evil, compromise with evil, and eventual participation in evil can happen not only in our personal lives but on a much larger scale as well. I saw this in a striking way in Rwanda.

After decades of tense and sometimes violent interactions, the dominant group in the culture, the Hutus, began to call the other ethnic group, the Tutsis, "cockroaches." To call someone a cockroach is initially humorous — what a silly thing to call someone! Makes you laugh. The popular radio stations used the term constantly, and eventually it became a derogatory way to refer to the Tutsis. Over time, the disdain many Hutus felt for Tutsis devolved into something more menacing. On the job, in schools, in fact, in every facet of society, the perceived distinctions between the two ethnic groups grew. The government issued identity cards that were used to promote racism. What began as name-calling turned into hostility in public life and then descended into outright hatred. "What should be done with cockroaches? You step on them!" It wasn't too many years before "cockroaches" were being murdered by fellow Rwandans.

It always starts so simply. If we don't hate evil, we laugh at it, compromise with it, and eventually accept it and participate in it. And those who don't speak up against it are as guilty as those who perpetrate it.

At this point, I wouldn't be surprised if your overwhelming response is "RUN!"

But don't run. Don't be afraid! This is not the time to run; this is the time to resist. Becoming aware of evil and choosing to stop ignoring it are decisions of the mind. Learning to hate evil engages our emotions; but actually resisting evil involves action. This is where you are called on to use every bit of your passion, energy, talent, and skill to actively push back the encroaching darkness.

Israel's great King David found consolation in God's comforting and strengthening presence: "Even though I walk through the valley of the shadow of death, I will fear no evil, for you are with me" (Psalm 23:4). God is with us, even as we walk through the valley of evil, the valley of the shadow of death! We do not need to be afraid — not because evil can't harm us, but because *God is with us* as we resist evil.

In every war there is a resistance movement, and they are almost always the fiercest fighters. These are the people who say, "Not on my watch! You may try to take over my country, but I won't go down without a fight." In World War II, the resistance fighters in France earned their heroic reputation due to their determination not to surrender their country to the forces of Nazism.

There is a war on evil occurring at this very moment. You and I must join the resistance and become the fiercest fighters against the evil surrounding us. I love J. R. R. Tolkien's Lord of the Rings saga because it's all about resistance.

This stirring trilogy showcases the clash of good and evil on an epic scale. In *The Return of the King*, the valiant hobbits, elves, dwarves, and those from the world of men do battle with the evil Sauron and his fiendish creatures. Every encounter is an attempt to push back the encroaching darkness. The hobbit and his friends are fighting against an evil that has more and better weapons and artillery, as well as gigantic monsters created for the purpose of inflicting colossal damage on living things as well as on man-made structures. They understand that all will be lost if they give up the battle — not just for themselves but for life as they know it. Yet the forces of good continue to resist as the forces of evil attempt to dominate. This is what resistance fighters do: even if they don't survive the battle, they fight. They stand. They give their all.

Most of us just can't be bothered with such depressing thoughts. We rationalize that evil isn't *that* bad. We don't pay much attention to evil until we encounter it personally or until we make a decision to stop being AWOL from the fight. This is a travesty.

Some of the most heroic people I know are engaged in exposing evil, opposing it, and doing what they can to push back the darkness. They are part of the resistance. Let me briefly tell you about some of them:

> • I am inspired and motivated to do my part by people like my friend Gary Haugen of the International Justice Mission. Gary was part of the United Nations team that investigated the Rwandan genocide in 1994 and now leads IJM to help countries enforce their own laws — laws against slavery, child prostitution, land

grabbing, and false imprisonment. Gary is using his skills and training as a lawyer to make a difference for thousands.

• My young friend Beth Waterman and others in Word Made Flesh live among the prostitutes of Calcutta and Chennai, India, helping women find meaningful lives and work outside of the darkness of the brothels. Her commitment to live among women with little hope for a good life shows me how to sacrifice myself on behalf of others.

• Pastor Stratton Gataha in Kigali, Rwanda, personally cares for those infected with HIV/AIDS in his congregation and has adopted children orphaned by AIDS or his country's genocide. Pastor Gataha and his wife, Adeline, are living out scriptural commands to prove the veracity of their faith by caring for orphans. Theirs is not a rich, comfort-filled life, but their obedience has brought them joy.

• Fulfilling a dream to go to Africa, Dan and Kathleen Hamer discovered that God had bigger plans than they anticipated. They put their arms around a five-year-old street child named Derrick in Kitale, Kenya, and bonded instantly. They eventually adopted not only Derrick but his younger brother, Reggie, also a street child. The passion on their faces is intense as they talk about the disgrace of millions of the world's children forced to fend for themselves on the streets of the world's cities. They won't rest until others join them in addressing the plight of these abandoned children.

• Heather and Scott Raines have adopted three special needs children — children truly on the bottom rung of society — from three different countries. Their adopted children need constant medical care and treatment just to survive, but the proud smile on Heather's face as she introduced each new little one to me touched something deep inside of me. These are her babies, loved as dearly as if they came from her own body. Heather and Scott's welcoming arms are pushing back the darkness.

• I am encouraged by politicians such as Senator Sam Brownback and relief organizations such as World Vision that use their influence on behalf of vulnerable children by teaming up to push for laws that make sex crimes committed by United States citizens in another country punishable in our country. Sex crimes against children are heinous and deserve to be punished. For years, predators have felt safe from prosecution at home, but now, because of Senator Brownback's and World Vision's tireless efforts, the bad guys have a harder time avoiding prosecution.

• I am in awe of the Christ-followers at Bennett Chapel Missionary Baptist Church in rural Shelbyville, Texas. In their small church of two hundred members, twenty-six families have adopted from the foster care system seventy children, many of whom have physical and emotional problems. These are not wealthy families, and they don't do it because it is a trendy thing to do. Pastor W. C. Martin and his wife, Donna, simply pointed out the biblical mandate to care for orphans, made it real by adopting three hard-to-place children themselves, and then encouraged others to care for these forgotten children. If tiny Shelbyville, Texas, can push back the darkness, so can the rest of us.

All of these individuals, organizations, and local churches are doing what they can to push back the darkness. They are willing to stop changing the channel and begin acknowledging the presence of evil — doing what they can with what they have to make a difference. They are willing to call evil evil — to expose it, oppose it, and try to end it.

The bad news is that evil is real and pervasive. You're in the crosshairs; it's coming after you too. But don't be frightened by that thought — it's just the reality of living in a world dominated by Satan and his followers.

The good news is that evil will not ultimately win. It may win some skirmishes, but it will *not* win the war. God will do away with evil completely one day: "The Son of God came for this purpose: to destroy the devil's work" (1 John 3:8 NCV).

Jesus came to destroy evil! Through his death and resurrection, Jesus broke the power of Satan, and one day evil will cease to exist. When Jesus comes back to reign as the King of kings, God will close the books of history on our bruised and broken planet. He will settle every score, punish evildoers, and banish Satan to hell where he belongs — forever.

Along with this guarantee, God's invitation to us is to transfer from being part of the darkness to being part of the light. Through a personal relationship with Jesus Christ, our hearts make a shift. We change allegiances. We become citizens of a new country — one that is far larger, better, and longer lasting than the country we now belong to. This citizenship transcends all earthly loyalties and ties and ethnic divisions and factions, and it will last into eternity. Here's how the Bible describes this shift:

> But you are not like that, for you are a chosen people. You are royal priests, a holy nation, God's very own —

possession. As a result, you can show others the goodness of God, for he called you out of the darkness into
his wonderful light.

1 Peter 2:9 NLT

For our citizenship is in heaven, from which we also
eagerly wait for the Savior, the Lord Jesus Christ.

Philippians 3:20 NKJV

As citizens of heaven, we have a mandate to expose
the darkness, oppose it with all our might, and use God's
extraordinary power to thwart its progress. Scripture is clear
about where our power comes from and how high the stakes
are:

> Only by your power can we push back our enemies;
> only in your name can we trample our foes.
> I do not trust in my bow;
> I do not count on my sword to save me.
> You are the one who gives us victory over our
> enemies;
> you disgrace those who hate us.

Psalm 44:5 – 7 NLT

This is no afternoon athletic contest that we'll walk
away from and forget about in a couple of hours. This is
for keeps, a life-or-death fight to the finish against the
Devil and all his angels.

Ephesians 6:12 MSG

It's easy to get demoralized by the weapons of darkness,
especially the visible ones — injustice, poverty, disease, cruelty, torture, rape, slavery, witchcraft, theft, adultery, murder, lying, corruption, abuse of power, false imprisonment.

Beneath the visible evil, we can see the invisible driving forces of evil — fear, superstition, greed, arrogance, perversion, hatred. The list could go on.

Most of us are ordinary people. We outgrew the fantasy of being superheroes a long time ago. There's very little about us that would qualify us as evil fighters. But we have access to the power of God, and the Bible says that God provides weapons that are not of this world. This means that no matter how intimidating evil appears, believers can stand boldly against it. How? By using the weapons God has given us.

Here is how the Bible describes the weapons at our disposal:

> We are human, but we don't wage war as humans do. We use God's mighty weapons, not worldly weapons, to knock down the strongholds of human reasoning and to destroy false arguments. We destroy every proud obstacle that keeps people from knowing God. We capture their rebellious thoughts and teach them to obey Christ.
>
> *2 Corinthians 10:3 – 5 NLT*

The God we've been talking about is himself good. It naturally follows, then, that those who know and love him will behave like he does. When his Holy Spirit is in control of our personalities and reactions, he will produce God's character qualities in our lives. As Paul writes, "The fruit of the Spirit is love, joy, peace, patience, kindness, goodness, faithfulness, gentleness and self-control. Against such things there is no law" (Galatians 5:22 – 23).

Jesus set the bar high for his followers: "Love your enemies, do good to them, and lend to them without expecting to get anything back. Then your reward will be great, and you will be children of the Most High, because he is kind to the ungrateful and wicked" (Luke 6:35 TNIV).

God's way of fighting evil has a surprising twist to it. We don't push back the darkness by using the weapons of evil but by using the "artillery" of heaven: truth, justice, holiness, dignity, honor, trust, fidelity, honesty, faith, hope, humility, sacrifice, duty, joy, gentleness, self-control, mercy, compassion, and *love*. It's tempting to lash out at evil with the same weapons evil uses, but doing so blurs the lines between evil and good. For instance, my knee-jerk response to the men who were abusing the little girls in Cambodia was to castrate them; I wanted to viciously maim them because of their perverted behavior. These men need to be arrested, prosecuted in a court of law, and then sent to prison — justice requires punishment — but my emotional desire for vengeance is not God's way.

You may be reeling from the examples of evil I've given, or perhaps the stories I've told remind you of the evil you or someone you love has encountered. You may find yourself horrified, angry, and perhaps even ready to rush out the door and pound on a few people. But if we're not careful, we will end up behaving just like the people we are trying to stop (more about that in the next chapter). For now, take your justified emotional response to God and determine to follow his marching orders: "Do not be overcome by evil, but overcome evil with good" (Romans 12:21).

The greatest weapon we have against evil is doing good in Jesus' name.

SURRENDER

Will you stop "changing the channel"
and living in denial of the evil in our world?

Prayer

Father, I confess to you that I have become very adept at changing the channel. Instead of pushing *back* the darkness, I push it *away* from me so that I don't have to acknowledge or feel the pain of living in a broken world. I've been living in a bubble of unreality. Will you move me to become angry about evil? I ask you to open my eyes to see evil, my ears to hear the cries of those being crushed by evil, and then my mouth to start speaking out on behalf of those who have no voice. I'm choosing today to begin to overcome evil with good. Please show me where to start.

SAY YES TO GOD

○ Pause right now and make a list of the evils in the world that particularly anger you. If you meet with a reading partner, share your list with this person and talk about it together.

○ Learn more about how others are pushing back the darkness by visiting some of the websites listed at www .kaywarren.com/resources.

○ Watch Kay's message "Pushing Back the Darkness" at www.kaywarren.com.

MIRRORS DON'T LIE

The heart is hopelessly dark and deceitful,
a puzzle that no one can figure out.
Jeremiah 17:9 MSG

Evil is not just where blood has been spilled.
Evil is in the self-absorbed human heart.
Ravi Zacharias, *Deliver Us from Evil*

I HAD HEARD THE GRUESOME STORIES OF THE GENOCIDE IN Rwanda in 1994. Over a period of one hundred days, approximately one million Rwandans were murdered by their fellow Rwandans in a manner that mimicked the genocidal frenzy that rocked Cambodia in the 1970s. Stepping off the plane at Kigali's small airport, I was sure I'd know how to spot them — how to look into the eyes of a Rwandan man or woman and evaluate whether or not they had participated in the genocide eleven years previous. I thought I would be able to recognize past criminal behavior just by talking to someone. I thought I would be able to identify those who betrayed husband, wife, child, aunt, uncle, neighbor, or fellow church member. How hard could it be to distinguish between the victimizers and the victims?

I was very naive.

Much to my chagrin, I couldn't tell by looking. I inter-
acted with men and women — Hutu and Tutsi — and unless
they told me their intimate life story, I had no way of figuring
out the good guys from the bad guys. This frightened me
and made me feel quite vulnerable. *I could be sitting across
the table from a murderer and not even know it*, I thought
to myself.

In one of the provinces, I met a city official — a nice-
looking man neatly dressed in a suit and tie. He gave us a
lavish welcome, served wonderful food under a tent that protected us from the sun, and delivered his official greetings.
But as we chatted and got acquainted, he quietly told me
and Rick in veiled terms that he had been part of the killings
in 1994. He alluded to his role but said it was very small.
Normally he would have expected to be punished severely,
but he said it was well-known that he was a good man who
had made bad choices in the passion of the moment. He was
granted leniency and a second chance to prove himself. I
remember listening to him talk while my mind raced with
his revelations. I instinctively recoiled; I wanted to pull away
and have nothing to do with him. What was the true extent
of his crimes? How could this ordinary-looking man have
been a part of the madness?

He didn't look like a monster.

Over the next few days, we visited the north, the east, the
west, and the south of Rwanda. We ate meals with pastors
and their families and met government leaders, businesspeople, poor people, well-to-do people, the sick and hospi-
talized, and those glowing with good health. I met regular
people who didn't look like monsters or behave like monsters; in fact, they seemed a lot like me. I was struck by how

normal everyone was. People were quietly going about their business, going to work, tending their crops, raising their kids—just doing life.

It slowly dawned on me. There weren't any monsters in Rwanda (or anywhere else, for that matter)—a special class of people for whom torture, rape, and murder came easily —but there were a lot of people like me: ordinary people who had gotten caught up in the hatred and passion of the moment and had allowed evil to reign in their hearts for a season. The implications of that realization stunned me into anguished reflection. Might I, too, be full of depravity, capable of committing the same atrocities if I were ever to allow evil to reign in my heart? This thought seemed too awful to accept.

God continued to fill in the shapes and colors on that piece of photographic paper he handed me in the spring of 2002. He had shown me that part of his plan for my life was to become an advocate for people with HIV/AIDS, and I had traveled to Africa and Asia to learn how HIV affects the lives of those it touches. Two bouts with cancer had shaken my faith and strengthened it at the same time. I had started the HIV/AIDS Initiative at Saddleback Church to inform, inspire, and equip our members to care for people with HIV/AIDS in our own community and around the world. The Global PEACE Plan was launched. Then came an invitation from President Paul Kagame for Rick and me to visit Rwanda.

In preparation for the trip, I pored over books about the genocide, watched several movies, and devoured anything I could find that would help explain what had happened there in 1994. As my knowledge of the genocide grew, I became outraged and horrified by all of the evil. I had gotten a taste of the effects of genocide in Cambodia, so as I anticipated going to Rwanda, I was hoping to expose evil and those who participated in it, no matter who was involved. I wanted *justice* for all who had been victimized by the terror that evildoers had inflicted on those weaker than themselves. I was on a mission to right the wrongs, seek punishment for the bad guys, and somehow make them pay for their behavior. In a word, I was full of righteous indignation and was feeling quite smug.

FACING THE EVIL WITHIN

The problem with my mission was that I had neglected to include myself in the list of evildoers. I was looking for monsters; what I found instead was the monstrous capacity for evil and wickedness in my own soul. I was so busy holding up a mirror to Rwandans and Cambodians that I couldn't be bothered to hold it up to myself.

The mirror doesn't lie.

Neither does the Bible. Scripture makes it clear that evil exists in our world; it exists in others, but it also exists in me — and in you. Evil is not just *out there*; it's *in here* — *in my heart* — and it's causing trouble. The Bible tells it like it is, exposing the evil hidden in all of us:

All have sinned and fall short of the glory of God.

Romans 3:23

So I find this law at work: When I want to do good, evil is right there with me.

Romans 7:21

You want what you don't have, so you scheme and kill to get it. You are jealous of what others have, but you can't get it, so you fight and wage war to take it away from them. Yet you don't have what you want because you don't ask God for it.

James 4:2 NLT

Temptation comes from our own desires, which entice us and drag us away. These desires give birth to sinful actions. And when sin is allowed to grow, it gives birth to death.

James 1:14 – 15 NLT

Here's how the Bible describes us in those verses: full of evil schemes, killers, jealous, fighters, trapped and stumbling sinners, full of useless self-confidence, prisoners of sin, lured by internal evil desires, people of sinful actions.

I have a feeling that, like me, you don't think of yourself in these terms. Those are words I use to describe the actions of others, not myself. In fact, you might be slightly offended that I would put us in the same category as people as heinous as Pol Pot, Hitler, Stalin, Jeffrey Dahmer, Hussein, or the ordinary citizens who became killers in Cambodia and Rwanda.

While it is true that it is much worse to commit an evil deed than to just be capable of doing it, we comfort ourselves too readily with that thought. As long as I put myself above anyone else, insisting that I would *never* do this or that, then I can excuse my own evil inclinations. The harsh reality is that, given the right circumstance, any one of us is capable of any deed.

Author Henri Nouwen describes it this way:

To care means first of all to empty our own cup and to allow the other to come close to us. It means to take away the many barriers which prevent us from entering into communion with the other. When we dare to care, then we discover that nothing human is foreign to us, but that all the hatred and love, cruelty and compassion, fear and joy can be found in our own hearts. When we dare to care, we have to confess that when others kill, I could have killed too. When others torture, I could have done the same. When others heal, I could have healed too. And when others give life, I could have done the same. Then we experience that we can be present to the soldier who kills, to the guard who pesters, to the young man who plays as if life has no end, and to the old man who stopped playing out of fear for death.[12]

Political campaigns, philanthropic efforts, common economic interests — these are fragile coalitions that disintegrate at the slightest challenge. They are not what unites us as human beings. Here is the truth that unites us: we are the same. Before we initiate God's love to hurting, suffering people, we must surrender our carefully cultivated illusions about the depth of our brokenness. We must admit that we are wretched and are completely unable to fix ourselves. By acknowledging our shared depravity and capacity for evil, we can reach out to a fallen brother or sister in mercy rather than in hatred.

I can hear you asking, "Why? Why does it matter if I've faced the evil inside of me? Why can't I just start caring and serving others, regardless of what's wrong on the inside of me?" This is an extremely important question.

As long as we refuse to look squarely into the mirror of

God's Word and get an accurate picture of ourselves, we actually do more harm than good. We must see ourselves, not as separate from others — better, more educated, more cultured, more sophisticated, more civilized, less sinful, less evil, less prone to violence, less likely to cause harm — but as identical to them in our capacity to do evil. Otherwise, we end up serving others from a position of pride, congratulating ourselves for our noble sacrifices rather than coming alongside a fellow stumbler and offering, not our wholeness, but our brokenness.

Some of us have a very difficult time acknowledging our sins, weaknesses, and failures. We either blame others for our problems or minimize our actions so that we can live with ourselves. We develop skillful ways to practice denial. There are also some folks who jump on the confession bandwagon and are willing to admit to theoretical sin or to sins they believe they've mastered. But it's a completely different thing to talk about *real* sin — specific and current sins we've committed that threaten to take us down today.

TEARING DOWN THE BARRIERS

I despise denial in other people — but I despise it most in myself. I am slowly learning how to be authentic and vulnerable, but I often get tripped up. I get caught in old patterns of relating, and I'm prone to blindness to my sin while focusing on Rick's sins or on the sins of someone I'm trying to minister to. Admitting my own sins, failures, and persistent weakness pulls down any barriers between me and another person.

As a little girl, I was molested by a young man in our church. My father was the pastor of a small Baptist church, and we thought we knew everyone. One adolescent had a secret: he molested children younger than himself. Eventually he was caught molesting kids in his neighborhood and sent to the California Youth Authority for several years, but the damage done to me lasted into adulthood. I never said a word, so my father had no idea that this young man had molested me. Because I was so young, I was unaware that my dad had tried to help this guy reestablish himself after he got out of the CYA. Years later, when I finally told my parents about the day that had caused so much brokenness in my life, they suffered tremendous agony. The fact that my dad had unknowingly aided the young man who wounded me added layers to the pain my parents experienced.

Sexual abuse is a complex subject with few easy answers or explanations, so it remains a mystery to me why I didn't tell anyone about the abuse. I did my best to block it out of my mind, but the effects of the trauma began to affect my developing sexuality. I became alternately fascinated and repelled by anything sexual and was drawn to the reference books on marriage that my dad kept on his library shelves. He had an early copy of Masters and Johnson's book *Human Sexual Response*, and I took every opportunity to devour what was written on those pages — secretly, of course.

The harm done to me continued to affect me as I grew into adolescence. I made many poor behavioral choices that plunged me into a cycle of temptation, acting out, and horrible guilt. Babysitting for neighbors gave me the chance to become addicted to the pornography I would never see in my home. Experimenting sexually with older friends became a regular part of my life for a period of time. All the while, the "good girl" part of me loved God passionately and wanted my life to count for something. The "bad girl" part of me didn't know how to break the cycle, and I learned how to compartmentalize myself. I convinced myself that I truly was a wonderful young woman, sincere in my faith and committed to Jesus Christ. At the same time, I didn't know what to do with this other person inside of me who did such shameful things. I tried to ignore her and then began to hate her. It never occurred to me that the sexual abuse at a young age had anything to do with my confused and frightened approach to sexuality.

Perhaps you can imagine what this compartmentalizing and denial did to my emotional and spiritual health. By the time Rick and I got engaged, I was totally messed up. I remember telling him casually one evening that I had been molested, but I was completely unemotional and didn't even shed a tear. Unfortunately, I didn't feel safe enough then to also tell him how it haunted me.

When Rick married me, he was unaware of the turmoil swirling deep in my soul because of repeated failure, guilt, and shame. We had an unusual courtship (a topic for another book!) and got married without knowing each other well at all. We were practically strangers. Our honeymoon was a disaster, and we returned from a two-week trip feeling devastated and heartbroken. Rick was a youth pastor in a growing church — who could we tell? We felt so alone. I was convinced our secret marital failure was too embarrassing to ever share with anyone else. We pretended that all was well, but month by month, our marriage deteriorated into a black pit. We were angry with each other, frustrated, ashamed, and afraid of intimacy. We grieved the loss of the cherished dream of a happy marriage. Over time, we have built a strong, stable, and healthy marriage, but it took an enormous amount of blood, sweat, and tears, along with great Christian marriage counseling.

Why am I telling you all of this? Because acknowledging secrets — not just the secret sins done *to me* but the secret sins done *by me* — allows me to identify with others who have fallen into the same traps.

I am rarely mindful of how self-righteous and judgmental I am, even though my family and closest friends have pointed it out to me over the years. It always stings when they mention it, and I usually do some fancy dance steps to dodge the accusation if possible.

But when I admit that I am sometimes full of rage and anger, then I can more easily minister to a man or woman guilty of taking that anger and rage one step further. When I own up to the fact that I have had embarrassingly shameful lustful thoughts for an inappropriate person, I can more easily minister to a man or woman guilty of expressing their secret lust. When I acknowledge I sometimes want more than is rightfully mine, I can more easily minister to a person who has stolen and gotten caught. Even more powerfully, when I confess I've not only thought of evil but participated in it, bridges are built between two people who really aren't much different after all. Suddenly, we both know why we need a Savior.

KNOWN TO THE DEPTHS
OF YOUR INMOST BEING

A few years ago while wrestling with the depth of evil I saw inside of me, I attempted to memorize Psalm 103. As I meditated on the first verse, "Praise the LORD, O my soul; all my inmost being, praise his holy name," I was intrigued by the phrase "inmost being." What does it mean to praise God with my inmost being? What is my inmost being?

Buried deep in the Guadalupe Mountains in southeastern New Mexico are the Carlsbad Caverns. From the outside, you would never suspect that subterranean caves fill the earth below your feet, one of them being so deep it is called "Bottomless Pit." I have come to believe that I resemble the Carlsbad Caverns. From casual conversation with me, you probably wouldn't know that deep inside of me are subterranean caves — layers and layers and layers of who I am. God in his amazing love and mercy enters into those caves of my inmost being, down into the deepest part of me where no other human being can enter, where no one else will ever know me. God enters into that place where there are no excuses, no pretensions, no false fronts, no hiding. *There* I cannot pretend to be anything other than what I really am and what I am not. *There* he sees completely the depravity of my heart in a way you will never see.

While watching the play *The Phantom of the Opera*, I was struck by the many ways we're all like the Phantom's tragic figure in our attempts to hide and deny our own brokenness. The Phantom is a twisted wreck of a man, horribly disfigured and totally alone, rejected even by the mother who gave him birth. He lives in the dark, dank caves underneath the Paris Opera House, and he secretly observes what goes on in the opera company. His soul aches for a companion, someone who will know him, accept him with his ruined face and warped soul. Over time, he falls in love with one of the beautiful singers, Christine, and schemes how he can bring her down into the subterranean caves. Even though there is an extremely high risk of further rejection, his longing for relationship and connection with another human being finally overcomes his fear, and he lures her to his hidden home. Her instincts alert her to the possibility that she will find something frightening there, so with great trepidation she follows him, descending lower and lower into the inky darkness. Her fears are well founded. Once she is deep in his cave, she is filled with terror and revulsion as the Phantom reveals just how broken and wounded he really is. In a panicked escape she abandons the Phantom. The pitiful sounds of his voice calling her name, begging her not to leave him alone in his misery, accompany her flight back to safety.

God is the *only one* who can enter deep into the caves of your inmost being and not be terrified or repulsed by what he sees. He was the only one who knew all along how wounded and broken I was on the inside. He was the only one who could meet me there with forgiveness, mercy, and healing. God saw all of the garbage — the shameful thoughts and behavior, the secret guilt and shame — that was ripping me up. Even now I would be tempted to put a bag over my head and go into hiding if other people really knew the depth of the ugliness inside of me. I don't know that I could look another person in the eye. But God, in his massive, almost unfathomable mercy, looked deep within me and said, "I love you, Kay. I know it *all*, and I still love you." He says the same to you.

"I know it *all*, and I still love you."

Because you are known at the deepest level by God — where your filthiest thoughts and most reprehensible deeds are revealed — and because you have been offered forgiveness and liberation through our Savior, Jesus Christ, you can authentically move toward the maturing knowledge that you're no different from the person living next to you. You need Jesus. I do too. *Everyone* does.

This truth changes everything.

Now we see why God instructs us to look in the mirror of his Word, because what we see there will keep us humble (see James 1:22 – 25). We are to let the Bible "judge" us — to point out our flaws, our sins, our failures, so that we can confess them and receive forgiveness. Once we've allowed God to "judge" us, we're more ready to "judge" the evil in our world. If that concept sets off alarm bells in your head, listen to what Jesus said in the gospel of Matthew:

> "Don't judge other people, or you will be judged. You will be judged in the same way that you judge others, and the amount you give to others will be given to you.
>
> "Why do you notice the little piece of dust in your friend's eye, but you don't notice the big piece of wood in your own eye? How can you say to your friend, 'Let me take that little piece of dust out of your eye'? Look at yourself! You still have that big piece of wood in your own eye. You hypocrite! First, take the wood out of your own eye. Then you will see clearly to take the dust out of your friend's eye."
>
> *Matthew 7:1 – 5 NCV*

Jesus' words here are often misunderstood and misapplied. I can't count the number of times I've heard folks drag out the phrase "Judge not, that you be not judged" to run from their own bad behavior or to paralyze someone trying to fight evil. Jesus isn't saying that judging other people is wrong — clearly our behavior is often deserving of judgment. What he is saying, though, is worthy of close attention. The new, higher standard he institutes is this: *The same yardstick you use to evaluate someone else will be used to evaluate you*; therefore, be careful how harshly you point a finger at another struggling human being unless you want that same finger to point back at you. Too often, when *my sin* is uncovered, I beg God for mercy and leniency; but when *your sin* is uncovered, I want God to throw the book at you.

But no longer. As Henri Nouwen suggests, a truthful look in the mirror will lead to something very different:

> By the honest recognition and confession of our human sameness we can participate in the care of God who came, not to the powerful but powerless, not to be different but the same, not to take our pain away but to share it. Through this participation we can open our hearts to each other and form a new community.[13]

You can begin to offer to others what you've received from God: forgiveness, grace, mercy, acceptance, second chances, new beginnings, "a crown of beauty instead of ashes" (Isaiah 61:3). You no longer have to live in denial of what you've done or what tempts you now. You don't have to pretend that you're better than anyone else and would never do what they've done. You're free — released to be a forgiven sinner who can forgive and accept others. Now you have something worth sharing! Instead of trying to fix someone — as though you have the perfect answer for every situation because you're perfect — you allow a connection to be formed. We share in our humanity and in our mutual need for salvation from evil.

Are you ready to begin to push back the darkness in yourself, in your home, in your neighborhood, in your city, your state, your country, your world? What will it require? Courageously surrendered people who are honest and bold enough to hold up the mirror of God's Word to themselves and ruthlessly examine their own motives and actions. God is searching for people who will confess their personal sin, accept his merciful forgiveness, and then humbly but boldly step into the battle against evil. When you and I minister to fallen fellow human beings with a realistic understanding of our own capacity to stumble, we bring not only truth and justice but healing and the possibility of compassionate redemption as well.

SURRENDER

Will you surrender your denial
about the depravity
of your soul and your ability
to do unspeakable evil?

Prayer

Father, you are a God who hates evil, no matter where it is found. I'm so grateful that you are also a God who loves to be gracious. Forgive me for denying and excusing my capacity for evil and wickedness. I have caught a glimpse of myself today, and I don't like what I see. I confess that I have screamed for justice when I've seen the sins of others, but I have begged for mercy when my own sins have been revealed. Please show me your grace. I am amazed that you see all there is to see in me — my inmost being — and you still loved me enough to send a Savior. Thank you for your kindness to me. The way you forgive me, mop up my messes, and repair the broken places over and over again is so humbling. May I be willing to give to fellow sinners the grace you've given me.

SAY YES TO GOD

○ Spend a few minutes praying and asking God, "What dark areas of my life are still hidden in the caverns?" If you have a reading partner and you're comfortable sharing these reflections, do so at your next opportunity.

○ Think about what God, in his unchanging mercy and grace, would say to you about these areas. Write out the words as if they were coming directly from God to you, and read them out loud to yourself.

○ Listen to a message by Kay titled "Overflowing Grace" at www.kaywarren.com.

THE GIFT
OF PRESENCE

"Look! The virgin will conceive a child!
She will give birth to a son,
and they will call him Immanuel,
which means 'God is with us.'"
Matthew 1:23 NLT

Compassion, to be with others when
and where they suffer and to willingly enter
into a fellowship of the weak,
is God's way to justice and peace among people.
Henri Nouwen, *Here and Now*

WHEN I THINK OF HEROES — PEOPLE WHO EMBODY COURA-
geous surrender — I think of Mother Teresa. Probably more
than anyone else in the twentieth century, she represents a
life yielded to God. She determined from an early age to allow
God to use her gifts, talents, and passions for his kingdom,
and what he did through this tiny woman is astonishing.

Because of my admiration for her selfless service to "the
least of these," I decided to visit her Home for the Dying
(Kalighat) in Calcutta, India, in October 2004. Not many
people have spent time in one of the Missionaries of Charity's homes around the world, especially non-Catholics, so

I thought I was doing something pretty wonderful. I felt noble, even virtuous, for what I was about to do.

There are two volunteer shifts a day at Kalighat, and my friends and I chose the morning shift. Volunteers are required to attend Mass with the sisters before beginning the workday. We knelt on the hard wooden floor of the Mother House and prayed, sang, and listened to the homily for the day with nuns in their white cotton saris. After tea and rolls, we headed to Kalighat. Once again, I was completely unprepared for the experience.

The sisters stay extremely busy tending to the women and men in their care — fifty on the men's side and fifty on the women's side — and don't have time for a cozy chat with new volunteers. When I asked one sister briskly walking past me what I should do, she barely glanced at me and said, "Do what you see others doing." I don't know if I expected her to stop, look me in the eye, and shower me with words of praise for showing up that morning, but it certainly wasn't the reception I anticipated! I noticed other volunteers grabbing gloves and surgical masks out of a metal bucket, but by the time I made it to the bucket, the only masks left were extra large — useless for me. Gloves? None that I could find. My friends Mary, Judy, Cisco, Steve, and I just looked at each other, and with a resigned shrug of our shoulders, we plunged into serving the dying men and women of Kalighat.

Steve and Cisco headed to the men's side, while Mary, Judy, and I went through the doorway for the women. Fifty small cots were lined up in rows, and there was a flurry of activity as volunteers, nuns, and patients mingled together. I quickly figured out that there was a system: women were fed breakfast, given a bath, and dressed in clean clothes; their bed coverings were changed; simple medications were dispensed; and then they sat on their beds or slept.

We joined the brigade of volunteers. Some of the volunteers come for weeks or months at a time, so there were a few veterans who took pity on our ignorance and gave us specific tasks to do: "Feed that woman over there. Be careful; she gets nauseated easily and throws up." "Here, help me get this woman into the bathing area. She can't walk by herself." "No, I'm sorry; there isn't any hot water to wash your hands. Just use that faucet and dry your hands on your pants." "Medication? Well, someone donated aspirin and a salve for fungus. The sisters are handing it out right now." "What is wrong with this woman? Maggots got into the wound on her head, and that awful-looking open sore is actually healing." "Clean that bed; no, there aren't any more gloves. Get some disinfectant from the kitchen and put it in that bucket of cold water. You'll find a piece of cloth that you can use to scrub the diarrhea off the mattress." "You really should put on a mask — the woman you're holding so close to your face probably has tuberculosis."

Within a half hour of arriving, my romanticized notion of "serving the poor" had evaporated into the stench of diarrhea and disinfectant and the screams of a man suffering as maggots are pulled from his wounds. The sight of injuries that made me feel sick and the stillness of a woman passing from this life into the next jarred me. "What a fool I am!" I thought to myself. Why did I want to come to this horrible place? When is my shift over? I can't wait to get out of here. I can't handle much more of this." I was a wreck.

LOVE THAT TRANSCENDS LANGUAGE

The morning routine was finally finished. Women were fed, bathed, and dressed in clean cotton dresses. Their beds had clean sheets. Some had received simple medicine, and now we waited — waited for them to die. That's what you do in a home for the dying.

I retreated to a quiet corner to gather my shell-shocked emotions and to allow my stomach to calm down from the sights, sounds, and smells. An alert nun saw me hiding and called for me to start folding donated newspapers into make-shift bags to dispose of soiled bandages. I am a klutz at art projects, and folding the newspaper in the precise ways the sister hurriedly demonstrated was harder than it looked. I was relieved that I could still be useful without interacting with any more women.

But then I saw her.

As my eyes wandered aimlessly, they met those of a woman sitting by herself on a cot on the other side of the large room. I silently scolded myself for making eye contact — hadn't I already earned my "nice person" stripes that morning? I felt as if all of my senses were on overload and I couldn't handle one more disturbing encounter. But she motioned urgently for me to come to her. I got up grudgingly and walked slowly to her side, where she drew me down on the cot next to her.

Instantly, tears streamed down her face, and in Bengali she began a torrential flood of words. My first thought was "I have absolutely no idea what she is saying," but then in a moment of clarity, I knew *exactly* what she was saying! This woman was pouring out her life story to me. She told me in the most vivid words she could muster how she ended up sick, alone, and dying in Kalighat. She mourned that her family was either too poor to care for her in her illness or too uncaring, or perhaps family had been lost long ago. I'm sure she told me of the hopes and dreams for her life that were dashed by circumstances and disappointments. Her grief grew by the minute, and her body trembled with emotion. We sat side by side on her tiny cot — an Indian woman approaching death and an American woman who didn't know how to help her.

All at once I was full of compassion for her, my sister.

I threw my arms around her and drew her very close to me so that our faces were just inches apart. While she was speaking in Bengali, I spoke in English, believing that the God who made her could help her understand, if not my words, the love with which I spoke them. "I am so sorry you hurt! I'm so sorry that you are here, alone and dying in this place. I'm so sorry that your family is not here with you — that they abandoned you to face your last days by yourself. But you are not alone! God is with you! You matter to him, and you matter to me. My arms around you are his arms; as I am wiping your tears away with my fingers, these are *his* fingers; as I touch your face, know that it is *his* hands lovingly reminding you of how dear you are to him. He loves you so much he sent his Son, Jesus, so that you could spend eternity with him! And he has sent me to you today to hold you and tell you one more time how special you are to him."

I couldn't assure her that she would leave Mother Teresa's Home for the Dying and be restored to full health. I couldn't guarantee her that her family would be outside, waiting joyfully for her to come home to them. I couldn't promise her that there would be adequate pain medication to make her death easy and comfortable. I offered the one thing I had in my power to offer — my presence, my very self. I offered her the gift that everyone can give — the gift that costs more than our money or even our energy and time — our very presence.

CONTAINERS OF GOD

Most of us are "fixaholics" — we see a need, and our first response is "Fix it!" I have to *do* something. Give me a fence to repair, a house to paint, a well to dig, a lesson to teach, a medication to dispense. Just give me something active to do! Those of us in the West are probably more prone to this response than people from other cultures. Our notorious self-reliance kicks in, and we rush to solve, to make it better, and to cure. There's nothing inherently wrong with fixing things, but it should *not* be our first response. Instead, we're to follow the model set for us when God saw our deep spiritual need for salvation.

God knew we needed a Savior to restore the ruined relationship between humanity and him. He set history in motion so that at the right time, he sent Jesus to be with us. He offered not just a plan or a strategy but a Person. He didn't send an angel; he came himself:

> So he became their Savior.
>   In all their troubles,
>   he was troubled, too.
> He didn't send someone else to help them.
>   He did it himself, in person.
>
> *Isaiah 63:8 – 9 MSG*

The Word became flesh and made his dwelling among us.

John 1:14

Throughout the Old Testament, God repeatedly reminded his children that he was with them. They weren't to be afraid of anything, because he was there. But they didn't quite understand. How do you relate to a God you can't see or touch or hear? God sent Jesus so that we would know what he is like:

Christ is the visible image of the invisible God.

Colossians 1:15 NLT

The Son reflects the glory of God and shows exactly what God is like.

Hebrews 1:3 NCV

Of all the gifts that God could give us, he gave the greatest one — he gave us himself. Now he expects us to do the same for others. As followers of Jesus, you and I are containers of God. We hold him within the fragile clay jars of our bodies. This is how the apostle Paul describes the light of God in us:

For God, who said, "Let there be light in the darkness," has made this light shine in our hearts so we could know the glory of God that is seen in the face of Jesus Christ.

We now have this light shining in our hearts, but we ourselves are like fragile clay jars containing this great treasure. This makes it clear that our great power is from God, not from ourselves.

2 Corinthians 4:6 – 7 NLT

Accepting Jesus Christ as Savior and Lord means that he comes to live within me. So I don't offer a new and improved "me"; I offer *him*. When I enter a room or any situation, I bring him with me because he lives inside of me. I don't just bring myself; I bring the God of the universe! In and of myself, I don't have much to offer to another person, but when I bring God, I've brought the one he or she needs the most. The Bengali woman in Kalighat needed to have the invisible God made visible to her.

How did he become visible to her? No blinding light flooded the room, no earsplitting trumpet blew, no thunderous voice blocked out all other sound. But by holding her in my arms, wiping the tears from her face, looking deep into her eyes, crying with her, and speaking of Jesus' unquenchable love for her, Jesus became real and visible. I made him real to her by being his hands and feet, by acting the way he acts, by loving the way he loves, by showing mercy and compassion, by giving the very best I had — Jesus Christ in me.

In the exodus God was *with* the Israelites, his presence represented by the pillar of fire and the cloud that led them through the wilderness of Sinai. But when the time was right, God came to earth in human form to be present with us. He sent Jesus to be *with us* in a whole new way. Jesus laughed at the antics of children, wept at the tomb of a cherished friend, bent to touch a leprous man, gently disciplined an outcast woman, and offered his life's blood for our sins. God with "skin" on him made truth personal and intimate. Now we believe it when Jesus says that God loves us. Jesus' life was an explanation of God. For us as Christ-followers, this is our primary task as well — to make the invisible God visible to a world that doesn't yet recognize him. We have the opportunity to *be with* another person in his or her need, thus "explaining" God. We are to live incarnationally

— God with us, God in us. To do so is at the heart of living our faith.

Once I understood this simple but profound concept of *presence*, I began to appreciate that every interaction with another person is a chance to treat people the way Jesus treated them. It's an opportunity to make the invisible God visible.

TOUCHING THE UNTOUCHABLES

In October 2004, I also traveled to the Philippines for the first time, and I asked to visit a leprosarium. Why would I be interested in leprosy? Well, for one thing, Jesus was interested in lepers! Second, the life of a leper closely mimics the life of a person diagnosed with HIV in the way leprosy affects a person physically, emotionally, and socially. Physically, leprosy and HIV attack the body in vastly different ways, but both decimate and destroy. Leprosy is a cruel disease — leaving those infected with permanent nerve damage. They have a loss of sensation in the affected part of the body, making it easy to become injured and not even know it. Burns, scrapes, bruises, cuts, and even breaks in bones occur with no pain sensation. The first sign that something is wrong is often gangrene, resulting in one's fingers, toes, or nose falling off. Wounds heal improperly or not at all. Scarring occurs where untended wounds heal in abnormal ways.

As has been true for thousands of years, lepers are still socially stigmatized and isolated, made to live apart from their families and friends. Many times they live in camps outside of the village, waiting to die. The fortunate ones are sent to a leprosarium for treatment. In the same way, people who are HIV positive frequently experience social stigma, rejection, abuse, and even persecution, leaving them with feelings of self-hatred and shame. In some cultures, it's not uncommon for husbands to beat their wives after they learn of their diagnosis. Neighbors refuse to let their children play with the children of a family in which someone is HIV positive. People with AIDS can lose their jobs if their status is known. Many have been asked to leave their church.

At the Manila leprosarium, the first ward we visited was full of men. Out of habit, I reached out my hand to greet a small, thin man in the bed closest to the door. He slowly raised his arm in response, and in a split second, I realized he had no fingers; a hand devoid of anything besides a stump was coming toward me. I'm ashamed to admit I had a knee-jerk response and fought the urge to pull my hand back. I had a conversation with myself in milliseconds: "Don't touch him. That's gross! OK, it's gross, but it's not that bad; you're just not used to seeing deformed bodies. Go ahead and shake his hand." I overcame my initial revulsion and warmly greeted him.

My interpreter and I then went from bed to bed, greeting and speaking to the residents. I learned that all of them had been cured of leprosy, but because of the deformities left by the disease, they were not welcome back in their villages. Some had lived in the leprosarium for twenty years, and it was home — they would never return to their families or their villages. Many were toothless, faces caved in where teeth used to be; most were missing fingers, toes, noses, ears, limbs — scarred and backs bent. We asked each one how we could pray for them and then held the stumps of their hands in ours as we asked God to meet their needs.

After a while, a small group of elderly women called the interpreter over and asked her why we were visiting. One tiny, gray-haired woman became the spokeswoman for all of them. She was incredulous that we would come — especially since we were Americans. She struggled to articulate her thoughts: "Why would you come here? Why are you touching us? Don't you know that we're yuck?" It reminded me of the lepers in Bible times who bore the shame of a terrifying contagious disease that required them to alert anyone near them of their "unclean" status. This woman believed that she and her friends were unclean.

My heart was pierced, and I spoke to her with some of the most powerful, healing words we can ever say to another human being: "You're not yuck! You matter to God, and you matter to us." She was disbelieving. Why would we soil ourselves by being with them, the outcasts? Why would we bother with these whom others ignore and reject? I went on: "God has not forgotten you; he has sent us to you today to remind you of how much he loves you!" She smiled, not quite accepting my words, but accepting the hugs we gave. Honestly, I had started the day feeling like they *were* yuck — my first reaction revealed my true feelings — but God gave me a chance, through the simple act of touch, to manifest his deep love for them as human beings of great worth.

Touching people who are sick, weak, and in pain or those who are scarred, maimed, and deformed — those whose bodies or minds are far from whole — validates their humanity. When we are willing to push past any fear, revulsion, or discomfort we may experience at the sight of their imperfection, we make God's presence real in this world; we make the invisible God visible to them. As the apostle John declared, "When you extend hospitality to Christian brothers and sisters, even when they are strangers, you make the faith visible" (3 John 5 MSG).

I returned to this leprosarium two years later to visit the friends we had made, and this time we brought magazines, candy bars, and lotion for dry skin. As we met with the director, we told him what we had brought, and his response touched me. "Thank you for bringing presents," he said. "The residents will appreciate them. But the greatest gift you can bring them is *your presence*." He put into words the truth I had come to believe, but it was awesome confirmation to hear a man who lived with lonely people every day express it in crystal clear words.

OFFER YOURSELF

As I was going through breast cancer, I found the greatest comfort, not in the verses of Scripture people sent me or the fantastic meals prepared by loving church members or the books on living with cancer; what comforted me was the *presence* of family members and friends who were willing to sit with me, sometimes without saying a single word. They brought the supernatural comfort of the Holy Spirit to my suffering just by *being with me*.

During my hospitalizations for chemotherapy, I found conversation intolerable most of the time. Every one of my senses felt heightened in unpleasant ways. Smells were nauseating; lights were too bright; sounds were amplified and echoed in my head; the cotton sheets were sharp and rough. I had dueling reactions — I just wanted to be by myself in my misery, and yet I didn't want to be alone. Rick would sit for hours near my bed, not saying a word. Sometimes he read; sometimes he worked on his computer; sometimes he napped — but he was always there. In the sweetest display of being with me, he chose not to preach any of the thirteen Christmas Eve services that year so he could stay home with me. If you're not a preacher, you probably won't see why this choice was such a big deal, but he lives for Christmas Eve and Easter. That's when all of the people who are seeking Jesus show up! For him to willingly and cheerfully forgo preaching at one of his favorite times of the year was the ultimate sacrifice. I loved him for choosing me over his ministry. He made a choice to be *with* me.

Job was a man whose suffering was intense; in a short space of time, he lost his children, his wealth, and his health. His bitter wife provided him no comfort; instead, she prodded him to "curse God and die" (Job 2:9). Comfort arrived when three of his friends showed up: "Then they sat on the ground with him for seven days and seven nights. No one said a word to him, because they saw how great his suffering was" (Job 2:13).

Job's friends did the right thing. When they saw the enormity of the suffering and sadness that had overcome their friend, they didn't try to speak words of comfort. They just sat by his side in silence; they were *with him*. Their presence on the ground next to Job spoke more eloquently about comfort, love, kindness, and compassion than all of their words put together. In fact, when they opened their mouths, they messed up! They began to analyze the reasons Job was suffering, speculating that he was holding on to secret, unconfessed sins. His companions' lack of understanding only increased his suffering. Their silent presence had brought him peace; the cacophony of their speech was bringing him pain.

As you've been reading this book, you may be discouraged by the enormity of evil and the vastness of the suffering of others, or maybe you're depressed at your own lack of power to change things. Let me share some good news: To make a difference, you don't have to have a grand strategy for eliminating poverty, HIV/AIDS, illiteracy, injustice, greed, or suffering. If you are a believer in Jesus Christ, you already have *within* you what it takes to bring relief, hope, and comfort to everyone you meet. You have Jesus inside you, and when you offer yourself, you're offering *him*.

You may be thinking, "I'm no Mother Teresa; I'm no saint." Contrary to popular opinion, I don't believe she was a saint, if *saint* means someone in a different class from the rest of us. If there aren't any monsters, then there aren't any saints either. *All of us* have the same capacity for evil and the same capacity for goodness as the next person. When we allow evil to control us, we do monstrous, shameful things. When we allow the Spirit of God to control us, we can love sacrificially in ways that seem beyond our ability to do so.

Henri Nouwen makes this wise observation:

> Every human being has a great, yet often unknown, gift to care, to be compassionate, to become present to the other, to listen, to hear and to receive. If that gift would be set free and made available, miracles could take place.... Those who can sit in silence with their fellowman, not knowing what to say but knowing that they should be there, can bring new life in a dying heart.[14]

When members from my church are preparing to go on

a short-term international mission trip, they frequently ask, "What will we do while we're there?" I tell them, "Perhaps the most important thing you will do is just show up." This isn't the answer they were expecting, and it isn't always a satisfactory answer. Some want to be given a list of activities and action steps. They want to be able to point to something concrete that they are leaving behind, a "proof" that they accomplished something significant during their time in another country. I understand this way of thinking — we all want to know that our investment of time, energy, and money has been worth it, that we haven't wasted our precious resources. What I'm suggesting is that in our hurry to *do something*, it's easy to rush past the people we're visiting. There will always be a need for action, for tangible solutions to complex problems. But as Christ-followers, let's be sure to *be with* people — to look them in the eye and listen to their stories, to spend a few moments entering into their experiences, whether joyful or painful. This is how the invisible God becomes visible.

SURRENDER

Will you offer to others
the greatest gift you possess —
God living in you?

Prayer

O God of all comfort, thank you for sending your Son to reassure me that life is not a solo journey. I'm amazed that you walk alongside me and that you intend to bring others to walk alongside me as well. Thank you, Jesus, for leaving all that was rightfully yours to give me the greatest gift I could ever receive—*your presence with me.* Today I surrender my reluctance to get involved with someone else in need—especially those whose bodies and minds are broken—and instead want to offer my presence. I'm available to sit in silence, to listen, to be with my friend without seeking to fix her, to give not my solutions but myself. Please live through me.

SAY YES TO GOD

○ Pause and quietly reflect on a time in your life when the presence of another person made a painful circumstance more bearable. If you have a reading partner, share the experience the next time you get together.

○ Decide to *really* listen to a family member or a coworker this week rather than letting your mind wander while they talk. Intentionally work on "being with" the people God brings across your path.

○ Watch the video "Straton's Story" at www.kaywarren.com. Don't hesitate to download it and share it with others.

A DELIBERATE CHOICE

Rejoice with those who rejoice,
and weep with those who weep.
Romans 12:15 NASB

The dying are moved by the love they receive.
Because of this, they believe that God
must be even kinder, more generous,
and so their souls are lifted up to God.
Sister Dolores, Missionaries of Charity

THAT NOW-BECOMING-FAMILIAR NERVOUS FEELING IN THE pit of my stomach started up, and my palms turned clammy. I glanced over at the young AIDS activist who had lined up the visit, and he gave me a slight nod as if to say, "Go ahead." My gaze returned to the faces of the patients who were staring at me. I shot a frantic look back at the young man, who now nodded more emphatically and muttered out of the side of his mouth, *"Go ahead!"*

"Go ahead with *what*?" I yelled inside my head. "This isn't what I expected. I don't have a prepared speech to give these people! Why does God keep putting me in situations for which I'm unprepared?"

As an HIV/AIDS advocate, I am always on a quest to learn

more — to get a good grasp on what the pandemic looks like in various parts of the world so that I can bring back the information and be a "translator" to others of what I've experienced. I realize that most people will not have the opportunity to visit the places I visit, so part of my task is to tell the stories of men, women, and children so that Americans can catch a glimpse of what it is like to live in Africa, India, Asia, Latin America, and Eastern Europe. I'm not a photographer or an artist, so I use words to paint pictures that convey the lives of fellow human beings who are suffering.

So here I was in Manila, having arrived at the AIDS hospice just moments earlier. I had expected to be visiting the patients one at a time, going from bed to bed to pray and offer encouragement. When we arrived, we had been shown into a small waiting room. Within minutes, I heard the shuffling sound of many pairs of feet coming toward me. Silently, a pitiful group of eleven men and women and two little boys filed into the room, many dragging rudimentary IV poles behind them. They sat down in a circle and waited expectantly for something — but what? I had no speech prepared; I thought I was going to be ministering individually to them — and I had no idea that two HIV-positive children would be there as well. Interacting with HIV-infected adults is one thing — but caring for HIV-positive children is much more poignant. They are so vulnerable — the most vulnerable of us all. The little boys were small and frail, with rashes on their arms and legs. Seeing the effects of a destroyed immune system displayed in their failing bodies filled me with sadness. They never smiled or warmed up to our playful gestures, preferring to huddle close to their parents.

In my panicked response to thirteen people bleakly staring at me, I did the only thing I could think to do in that moment — I asked if we could pray for them. Through the translator, they gave their permission for us to hold their hands and pray. I feebly asked, "How can we pray for you today?" One man — whom I had guessed to be a woman — spoke up loudly in English. "The pain! The pain! Oh, the pain! I can't stand the pain!" He rubbed the tops of his thighs wildly. "I just want to die. I don't care if I go to heaven or hell; I just want the pain to stop!" His passionate cries stunned me into silence. Any words I might have said died in my throat. Then I began to look around the circle to see how the other patients were reacting to his gut-wrenching admission of pain. Tears were coursing down every cheek except for those of the two little boys, whose faces were blank and withdrawn.

I threw one arm around the man who was in pain, held tightly to the hand of another patient on my other side, and began to pour out my heart to God on behalf of these new friends:

> God, we have come here today to remind our friends that you love them, that you have not forgotten them and will never abandon them. We may never see each other again on earth, but for this one day, we have come to help carry their load of pain, suffering, and sadness. We take their pain as our own and weep with them. We beg you for mercy. Would you bring relief from this terrible aching and hurting? Would you cause the medications to work effectively? Jesus, their pain is not a mystery to you; you know every place on their bodies that hurts, the parts that don't work properly and have grown weak.

Would you help them sleep peacefully tonight, knowing you are at work in their bodies? Would you bring us to their minds from this point on when they start believing they don't matter? Would you remind them that just as we have come to carry their pain for a day, you want to carry it *every* day? Thank you that this life is not all there is, but that we have hope for another life in which pain, suffering, sadness, disease, and sorrow will be gone.

That prayer, spoken in a whisper, opened the door to tender encounters with each person in that room. When I finished praying, our team instinctively reached out our arms to these people who were in various stages of dying. They had been silent or reserved in their response to us, but suddenly our tears mingled with theirs and our arms were entangled with theirs, and they pressed their bodies close to ours, drinking in the comfort of physical touch.

I have learned that sick people are usually starving for touch. An arm draped around their shoulders, a kiss planted on their cheek, a warm handshake — all of these things let them know in tangible ways that they are indeed still lovable, valuable, and worth something. Jesus showed us how to do this. He put his arms around the children and drew them near. He touched the leprous man and healed him. He looked the adulterous woman in the eye and reminded her that she still had value, even though her behavior made her an outcast. Physical touch conveys acceptance and love in profoundly significant ways. It says, "I care deeply about you."

That day we chose — deliberately, unreservedly, and willingly — to take on the pain of people we had never met and would probably never see again. We chose to take within ourselves the agony they were experiencing and to let it wound us. Compassion is choosing to share the pain of another. To do so runs counter to our natural inclination to protect ourselves from pain. It requires self-sacrifice and obedience to Jesus — as we do for others what he did for us.

CHOOSING PAIN

God could have merely sent Jesus to be with us in our humanity, to walk with us, to see life through our eyes, and to stand next to us in our pain and suffering. It would have been more than we have the right to expect of God. But God didn't stop there; he asked Jesus to go even further and actually suffer our pain. Jesus took our suffering on himself. He didn't just nod sympathetically when we were lost and dying in our sin or shed tears of empathy when we cried. He saw our pain and willingly chose to bear it on his shoulders, to carry it in his heart, and even to take our sin on himself and die in our place. He let our wounds wound him. This is "suffering with" — a deliberate choice to embrace pain that is not your own. The apostle Peter put it this way: "He personally carried our sins in his body on the cross so that we can be dead to sin and live for what is right. By his wounds you are healed" (1 Peter 2:24 NLT).

The prophet Isaiah summarizes this thought in powerful language:

> But he took our suffering on him
> and felt our pain for us.

We saw his suffering
   and thought God was punishing him.
But he was wounded for the wrong we did;
   he was crushed for the evil we did.
The punishment, which made us well, was given
     to him,
   and we are healed because of his wounds.
We all have wandered away like sheep;
   each of us has gone his own way.
But the LORD has put on him the punishment
   for all the evil we have done....
For this reason I will make him a great man among
     people,
   and he will share in all things with those who are
   strong.
He willingly gave his life
   and was treated like a criminal.
But he carried away the sins of many people
   and asked forgiveness for those who sinned.

Isaiah 53:4 – 6, 12 NCV

Once again, Jesus' way of making the invisible God visible to us shows us how we are to respond to the pain of another. As Isaiah declared, "[Jesus] took our suffering on him and felt our pain for us. We saw his suffering and thought God was punishing him. But he was wounded for the wrong we did." Don't let mental pictures of the awful bloodiness of the cross blot out the splendor and beauty of what Jesus did for you. Somebody loved you enough to take your suffering on himself. Somebody was willing to let what was crushing you crush him. As his bond slaves — those who serve the Master out of love, not duty — we, too, move into our neighborhoods and cities looking for those who are being crushed and broken by suffering and offer to *suffer with* them.

Author Lewis Smedes reminds us that we all suffer in this life, sometimes because of our own actions and sometimes because of the actions of others — a suffering *from* situation. Smedes invites us to become radical in our suffering by choosing to suffer *with* another person:

> So much for being victims of suffering. We need to get on with the heart of the matter: voluntary suffering. Suffering *with* people! We suffer with people when we choose, freely, to let their hurts hurt us. Forget about being a victim; here you decide for yourself whether you want to be hurt or not. We are free in this suffering — free to suffer or to run, free to take on pain, and free to say NO to it.
>
> We do not hurt now because nature whops us, we hurt only because we choose to share the hurt nature lays on other people. We bring it on ourselves, it is our doing. We make our move, get close to sufferers to let their pain seep through their skins into our hearts until their pain becomes our pain. Here, in the irony of chosen pain, we volunteer to accept a pain we want to do without; we volunteer to be hurt with a hurt we would rather not feel; we volunteer to bear a burden we want very badly not to bear. This is voluntary suffering. It is the last word in love's power to move toward our neighbors — not to get pleasure from them, but to get hurt with them....
>
> In suffering *with* somebody, we take it into our own hands to suffer. We choose to do what we do not have to do, or even want to do; we walk, eyes wide open, into the pain of another human being and claim it as our own.[15]

Did you catch that last line? We are to walk with our eyes wide open into the pain of another human being and *claim it as our own.*

PROMPTED TO MAKE A PROMISE

Don, a gay man recently diagnosed with AIDS, was involved with an AIDS services provider in Orange County. The HIV/AIDS Initiative at Saddleback was interested in learning how we might assist some of their clients. He asked for a tour of Saddleback, so we met on the church campus and walked around for about an hour, ending up in my office for a chat. Like some of those I meet who are active in caring for people with HIV, he was cordial but not overly friendly at first. Evangelicals — including those in my church — have largely been absent from the fight against HIV/AIDS, and some folks are suspicious and wary when we show up twenty-five years later and tell them we would like to serve with them. I understand this and feel no defensiveness about their reticence. Don was merely reflecting back to me the attitude of others who have felt the sting of rejection and outright hatred.

When he asked me to tell him how I became an advocate for people with HIV/AIDS, I went through my journey, including breast cancer. Our eyes locked as I said to him, "I am not HIV positive, so I don't know what it's like to be you. But I have received another kind of life-threatening diagnosis, and without medication, breast cancer would eventually kill me. I've faced death in new ways, and I've discovered I'm not as afraid to die as I used to be." He touched my hand as it rested on the table and said, "I'm not afraid to die either; I just don't want to die alone." He articulated the fear that all of us face — the dread of dying alone.

Don opened his heart to me that day and shared some vulnerable and authentic feelings. I was amazed that a complete stranger and I could establish a connection so quickly — and it all happened because we both knew what it was like to face death. I had to restrain myself from blurting out the words that were on the tip of my tongue — after all, we didn't know each other — but I felt instantly that the Spirit of God was prompting me to make a radical, if not completely illogical, commitment to Don.

I chickened out while we were together, but later that night, I sent him an email and told him that I wanted to make a commitment to him that he could count on. Here's part of what I wrote:

Even though we don't know each other well at all, I was so moved by the vulnerability of what you shared with me today. I would like you to know that I'm promising that, to the best of my ability, you won't be alone when you die. You probably have other friends and family members who will be near you and with you, but now you have one more.

This was so out of the blue. Reasonable people don't promise to be next to a dying person in advance of their death — especially when the person is a total stranger. I had never done anything so rash and so — *weird*. Somehow in the depths of my heart I knew that God was directing me to make this promise to Don. I didn't have any idea how he would respond, but he wrote back a long, emotional email message that thanked me for caring so deeply for him.

We began a friendship. He and his partner visited Saddleback on Mother's Day (of all days), and we made plans to get together again soon. But almost as quickly as he came into my life, he went out of it. His illness progressed to the point where he had to quit his job, and he then told me he was moving out of the area. He gave me his new email address and contact information, but he stopped writing, and I lost contact with him. This turn of events was very confusing. I prayed, "God, I know you brought Don into my life. He showed me how to connect with another person on an emotional level and how to minimize our different beliefs until we could establish a relationship. I thought you were asking me to be with him for a long time; to get to know him, to learn to love him, and to stay with him as a friend until he passes away. But now he's gone and is making no attempt to stay in contact. Did I misunderstand what you told me?"

God has not yet answered my questions about Don — but I meant what I said. God had prompted me to be willing to take on the pain of another human being and carry it within myself all the way to the end — even if "the end" meant I would carry his pain until he died. I had made the choice to *suffer with*.

LOVING JESUS BY LOVING OTHERS

One day, Jesus caught his unsuspecting disciples off guard with a "compliment." I suspect they were initially pleased by his words of apparent commendation but then became completely confused as they tried to figure out what he meant: "For I was hungry, and you fed me. I was thirsty, and you gave me a drink. I was a stranger, and you invited me into your home. I was naked, and you gave me clothing. I was sick, and you cared for me. I was in prison, and you visited me" (Matthew 25:35 – 36 NLT).

I can imagine the puzzled looks on the disciples' faces as they question Jesus: "Lord, are you sure you're thinking of the right disciples? We don't remember feeding you when you were hungry or visiting you in prison. We sure don't recall you being naked and us giving you some clothes. Were you ever sick? Must have been when you got up early and went to the other side of the lake. We think you're getting your facts mixed up." And Jesus responds with those unforgettable words: "Whatever you did for one of the least of these brothers and sisters of mine, you did for me" (Matthew 25:40 TNIV).

Most of us stop there in the biblical narrative. Jesus' words are already convicting because we realize how little we've done for the sick, the poor, those in prison, the homeless. But then he takes it one step further:

> "Then the King will turn to those on the left and say, 'Away with you, you cursed ones, into the eternal fire prepared for the devil and his demons. For I was hungry, and you didn't feed me. I was thirsty, and you didn't give me a drink. I was a stranger, and you didn't invite me into your home. I was naked, and you didn't give me clothing. I was sick and in prison, and you didn't visit me.'
>
> "Then they will reply, 'Lord, when did we ever see you hungry or thirsty or a stranger or naked or sick or in prison, and not help you?'
>
> "And he will answer, 'I tell you the truth, when you

refused to help the least of these my brothers and sisters, you were refusing to help me.'

"And they will go away into eternal punishment, but the righteous will go into eternal life."

Matthew 25:41 – 46 NLT

Do you get it? Jesus tells the disciples that they have made two huge mistakes: they haven't taken care of those in need, and by failing to take care of them, they have failed to take care of *him*.

The bottom line "proof" of our love for Jesus is a surprising measurement. It's not found in the ways we've typically used to evaluate our spiritual maturity. Proof of our love for Jesus is found not merely in attending church, reading the Bible, singing praise songs, being part of the choir, teaching a Sunday school class, or serving as an usher or an elder (although each of those activities is an important part of a growing spiritual life), but in loving and serving the sick, the poor, the weak, and the marginalized.

You can't physically give Jesus shelter, fix him a meal, or put a clean shirt on his back; you can't visit him in a prison cell or offer him a drink of water. But when you do it for *them* — for the least — you are doing it for him. And when you're *not* doing it for them, you're *not* doing it for him.

Ouch.

This teaching was brought home to me in a powerful way during the visit to Mother Teresa's Home for the Dying in Calcutta. It seemed as though everywhere I looked in the "Mother House" (where the Missionaries of Charity live and have their chapel services) and in the Home for the Dying, there were crucifixes on the walls with a plaque above them that read, "I Thirst." Mother Teresa had these words affixed to the crucifixes as a constant reminder to the sisters and the volunteers *why* they were serving the poorest of the poor.

You and I cannot go back in history and give Jesus a drink of water to quench the thirst he experienced as he hung on the cross, but we can certainly quench the thirst of the "least of these" on a daily basis. I cannot stop the pain Jesus felt while the nails ripped his flesh, but I can kneel next to a woman in excruciating pain and wipe her brow. I cannot cover Jesus' naked body, left exposed to ridicule by soldiers, but I can clothe a child whose only shirt is torn and filthy. If, as Mother Teresa said, Jesus is seen in his "most distressing disguise" of the poor, then when I meet their needs, I am offering love to my Savior. Conversely, when I do not choose to meet their needs, I am neglecting him.

Deliberately choosing to enter into the experience of a fellow human being sets the stage for God to make an entrance. As Sister Dolores, a member of the Missionaries of Charity, says, "The dying are moved by the love they receive.... Because of this, they believe that God must be even kinder, more generous, and so their souls are lifted up to God."[16] Choosing to *suffer with* proves our love for our Savior and at the same time proves to the least, the last, and the lost that there is a Savior who loves them.

I've never lost a child to AIDS, but I feel the pain of millions of mothers and fathers who have. I've never buried a husband, but millions of women have. I've never been pushed out of my home and community because of a health diagnosis, but millions of people have. I've never faced the agonizing decision about whether to breastfeed my children and expose them to HIV, or whether to formula-feed them and perhaps expose them to germs that can kill them just as easily, but millions of mothers have. I've never watched my children digging through rotting garbage to find their next meal, but millions of mothers have. I've never sent a son or daughter to war, but millions of parents have. I've never spent a night on the street hoping no one takes my few belongings while I sleep, but millions have. In each case, when I feel their pain, their anguish, their despair, I am choosing to carry their burden with them. Choosing to *suffer with* is a powerful witness to being a Christ-follower. He chose to suffer with me; I can now choose to suffer with a fellow human being for Jesus' sake.

Are you beginning to understand that compassion is about making a decision? It's not an emotion that hits you out of the blue; expressing compassion is a deliberate choice. When you stop changing the channel and stop denying evil and suffering, you can begin to cultivate some new habits, some new Christlike patterns of response. We are most like Christ when we *choose* to offer the gift of our presence and *choose* to absorb within ourselves the suffering of the least, the last, and the lost. Are you looking for Jesus? That's where you'll find him.

SURRENDER

Will you freely choose to bear pain
that is not your own?

Father, thank you for sending Jesus not only to
be with me in my pain but to take my pain on
himself. Lord Jesus, how grateful I am that you
were willing to bear my pain and the penalty
of my sinful choices; willingly you let it all be
poured out on you. Give me the courage it takes
to choose to suffer *with* another human being;
give me the strength I will need to bear not only
my own suffering but theirs as well. Please love
through me. May I enter into the life of another
so completely that I laugh uproariously when
she celebrates and weep uncontrollably when she
grieves. In my laughter and tears may she hear
your joy and know your compassion. Please love
through me.

SAY YES TO GOD

SAY YES TO GOD

○ Pray for someone you know who is suffering, asking God to let you *feel* some of what he or she is experiencing. If you have a reading partner, spend time together praying about these situations.

○ Take a meal to someone who recently lost a loved one; make a hospital visit to someone who can use an encouraging word; offer to be with your neighbor's chronically ill child so she can spend a much-needed evening out with her husband; write a note or an email to someone who is depressed and doesn't know which way to turn.

○ Listen to Kay's message "Why Should I Care?" at www .kaywarren.com.

AN UNEXPECTED BOND

God will do this, for he is faithful to do what he says,
and he has invited you into
partnership with his Son, Jesus Christ our Lord.
1 Corinthians 1:9 NLT

The measure of the worth of our public activity for God
is the private profound communion we have with Him.
Oswald Chambers, *My Utmost for His Highest*, January 6

ONE HOT AFTERNOON, OUR GROUP CAREFULLY PICKED OUR way through a teeming side street near the Temple of Kali in Calcutta, India. Lining both sides of the street were alleyways, one after the other. In each alley entrance, women of various ages slouched against the walls. Some of the women were dressed seductively, others elegantly, still others in rags. Prostitutes. Streetwalkers. Ladies of the night. Women of ill repute. Whores. The politically correct term is *commercial sex workers*. I had never spoken to a prostitute before — not in the United States and certainly not in another country. But on this particular day I was surrounded by them.

Let's be honest: prostitutes rank near the bottom of the social ladder. They're fodder for late-night TV jokes and Hollywood film material, and their mention can cause errant politicians and TV evangelists to sweat bullets. But nobody treats them like human beings. I grew up believing that women became prostitutes for one reason: they were slimy people. I confess I didn't really want to get to know prostitutes, but in my gradual maturation as an HIV/AIDS advocate, it became clear that sex for money is one of the driving forces behind the AIDS pandemic. If I was going to make sense of the ways in which commercial sex workers affect the spread of HIV, I needed to put a face to the millions who live as prostitutes. Each step of my journey into courageous surrender has held startling lessons, and the lessons have usually come through the "least of these" — those who are vulnerable, despised, and rejected by polite society.

I discovered that a growing number of compassionate followers of Jesus Christ have allowed their hearts to become tender toward the women and men in the global sex industry and are actively seeking ways to minister hope, healing, and a way out in Jesus' name. After all, when given the opportunity to slam a woman caught in sexual sin and another woman notorious for being a prostitute, Jesus treated both with dignity. He didn't condone their sinful behavior, but he was kind and respectful in his interaction with them.

He treated them like human beings.

APPEARANCES CAN BE DECEPTIVE

One wonderful couple living among the brothels of Calcutta brought me and my friends Judy and Mary to meet a few of the women with whom they were developing friendships. They walked with us down that side street filled with prostitutes.

Coming out of the side street onto the main road, with cars, buses, bicycles, and throngs of people passing by, we attracted attention. Even though we had covered our heads and were wearing the loosely fitting pants and oversized blouses common to poorer Indian women, there was no disguising our skin and foreign appearance. People stared, nearly crashing into each other as they craned their necks to look at the strange women talking to the prostitutes plying their trade. To avoid creating more of a scene, we persuaded three of the women to get in a taxi with us and drive a short distance to a small tearoom where we could talk. Our missionary friends had refurbished it and were using it as a place where the women could go without being harassed.

The room was freshly painted and furnished with just a small table and chairs, but the three prostitutes refused the chairs and sat on the ground with their backs against the wall. I felt awkward sitting on a chair while they sat on the floor, so I moved to the mat next to them. One of the women instantly shifted from hugging the wall to hugging me. She intertwined her arm with mine, grabbed my hand, and tightly squeezed my fingers. Her slender body was pressed up to mine, and her head rested on my shoulder. When my body shifted, hers shifted in response. She looked up into my face as we talked, and she giggled and chattered constantly, seemingly unconcerned that we weren't speaking the same language. We sat tangled together until my back ached and my legs and feet were deadened. I wanted to stand up and shake my sleeping limbs, but I sensed a holy connection developing between us. Something sweet was happening in a spiritual dimension, and I was reluctant to interrupt it.

At first, all of the women laughed easily and joked among

themselves. I'm sure they were making fun of our ugly, shapeless garments that paled in comparison to their brilliantly colored silk saris woven with golden threads. Their bodies were on display, and ours were covered up. They were seeking attention, and we were trying to blend in. As we got acquainted through an interpreter, they told us about their children, their villages, their lives in Calcutta, their HIV status, and their stories of how they became prostitutes.

This topic brought serious expressions to their faces as they told us their stories. A husband sold one of them into prostitution; another woman's aunt sold her; the third was sold by a neighbor. All laughter and silly playfulness faded for good when I asked them how they remained joyful in such circumstances. Tears spilled onto their lovely faces. "Joy? My joy ended the minute I came here from my village," said one. "There is no joy." We sat in silence for a few moments trying to absorb the horror of their lives. I couldn't stop myself from asking the obvious question: "Why don't you leave? Why don't you just stop being a prostitute?" They replied as one: "What would we do? We have no skills. How would we live? Our families are expecting the money we earn. There is no escape."

I breathed a silent prayer:

God, forgive me for looking only at the outward appearance of these women. They look cheerful and content; their physical beauty is astounding. How could I be so dense as to think this is the life they would have chosen for themselves? Of course there is hidden pain. They were betrayed by someone they trusted and *sold* like a piece of pottery, treated like a commodity instead of a human being. You know this pain, Jesus. You were betrayed and sold out by a friend. You experienced the stabbing thrust of being abandoned and used. These women see a dead end ahead of them—no way out. They can't go back to being innocent young women in their villages, and they can't think of any other way to support themselves at this moment. Would you please love them through us right now? May they comprehend— even though we don't speak the same language—that you love them so much that you died for them?

There were profound spiritual truths hidden in that encounter with these outcast women. All I could see at the time was that God and I shared a love for them. I didn't realize how close they brought me to him and how being with them deepened my fellowship with Jesus. It would take a time of depression and reflection to recognize how suffering with others brings us nearer to the heart of God.

THE FELLOWSHIP OF SUFFERING

I traveled extensively during the summer and fall of 2004, visiting Thailand, Cambodia, the Philippines, and India. If I had been seriously disturbed and gloriously ruined by my visits to Mozambique, Malawi, and South Africa a year earlier, what I witnessed in Asia and Southeast Asia launched me into a deep depression from which I couldn't find a way out. The depression was probably the culmination of battling cancer, undergoing the treatments, and having had all kinds of jarring experiences after reading the magazine article in the spring of 2002.

All I know is that after my trip to the Philippines and India, I found that I couldn't stop crying. I couldn't sleep. Nothing excited me or interested me. The faces of the men, women, and children troubled me, and their suffering threatened to bury me. The enormity of poverty, AIDS, ignorance, genocide, orphans, widows, injustice, and hatred, piled on top of my own suffering, siphoned away any joy or pleasure. Sadness and grief morphed into apathy and listlessness, and my default mode became hopelessness.

I had been angry at God when going through cancer treatments — angry that he allowed such a broken world to even exist.

Now I was not angry; I was flattened.

Several of those who traveled with me were experiencing this same kind of hurt. We talked often, comparing notes and looking for signs that relief was on the horizon. I just wanted to feel like myself again. After about six weeks with no movement toward normalcy, I called our missions pastor, Mike Constantz, and asked for advice. He suggested that my friends and I come pray with him and a few other pastors who had missions experience. They knew firsthand how traumatic this exposure to evil, pain, and suffering can be, especially for those who have lived rather sheltered lives.

We gathered around a large table, Bibles and journals in hand, hoping against hope that they had answers for our pain. Pastor Mike read a powerful passage of Scripture: "I want to know Christ and the power of his resurrection and the fellowship of sharing in his sufferings, becoming like him in his death" (Philippians 3:10).

He firmly but gently said, "Every time your heart breaks for a child orphaned due to AIDS, know that God's heart is breaking at the same time. Every time you cry when you are with a dying man or woman, know that there are tears on God's face as well. When you think you can't stand the pain one more second and want to wipe out all of the evil in the world, know that God's passion to destroy evil is even greater. You now get to taste just a portion of the anguish God feels about our broken world. If you let it, this will bring you into a deeper communion with him as you begin to share in the sufferings of Christ. He suffers for our world. Now you have been allowed the privilege of joining in his pain and sorrow. You and Jesus will weep together."

Pastor Mike's insights opened up a whole new realm of thought and understanding for me. I had never quite comprehended what the Bible means when it says there is fellowship — kinship, community — in sharing the sufferings of Jesus. Frankly, it had always sounded way too mystical, even for a mystic like me! But through the haze of my depression and numbness, I grasped that my current hope of obliterating the pain was not the way out of distress. God had something better in mind. In the emotional agony I was feeling, God was inviting me to draw nearer to his heart than I ever had before. He was welcoming me into *his* world — to let my painful reaction to suffering take me deeper into intimacy with him by feeling what he feels.

Have you ever wondered how God *feels*? Has it ever crossed your mind to ponder how God *feels* about murder? Rape? Incest? Adultery? Torture? Poverty? Stigma? Sickness? Injustice? From even just a rudimentary look at the Bible, we can say for certain that God hates all of them (Proverbs 6:16 – 19)! He gets angry at the devastation that sin has caused on our planet (Isaiah 61:8). The New Testament records Jesus' weeping over the people of his beloved Jerusalem when he saw their oppression (Matthew 23:37), his crying at the news that his friend Lazarus had died (John 11:35), his anger when businesspeople tried to cheat worshipers at the temple (Matthew 21:12), his wrath when religious leaders cared more about observing the Sabbath than they did about a woman broken by illness (Luke 13:10 – 17), and his fury that adults would ever wound a vulnerable little child (Luke 17:2).

Our God *feels* deeply and passionately.

It should have come as no surprise, then, that if I was going to love God deeply and passionately, it would automatically lead to a broken heart for me. There's no way to grow in loving him and not grow in having his heart for his world, leading directly into his sufferings. Radical internal changes occur when we become Christ-followers, and the changes will eventually spill over externally into how we live our lives. Identifying with his cross and his resurrection will alter how we spend our brief years on this earth. What we do and where we go; how we spend our money, time, talent, and energy; and how we respond to people in need are all determined by how deeply we enter into the fellowship of the sufferings of our Savior.

This is a good thing! It's nothing to be avoided. Caring about what he cares about permits us to actually share in *his* passion, and in so doing, we find soul-building fellowship. Jesus' pain is to blend with my pain, his tears with my tears, his wounds with my wounds; his cross is to become my cross, his comfort my comfort.

As François Fénelon observed, there is a beautiful uniting of our hearts with Christ's when we suffer together: "When you love God, it will not matter to you what you must suffer on His behalf. The cross will make you over in the image of your Beloved. Here is real consolation — a true bond of love."[17]

Through my depression, I discovered that I had gotten caught in the subtle temptation common to caring individuals, summarized in these words: "Take on the world by yourself." When my heart was broken for people with HIV/AIDS, the "go get 'em" mentality took over, and I dove headfirst into attempting to single-handedly save the world from the effects of this dreadful virus. I often felt as though it all depended on my efforts, my work, my compassion. True, I never *said* that, and I'm not sure I was even conscious of how thoroughly I had given in to a "savior complex," but the effects of it were obvious in my life.

It reminds me, in a significantly smaller, much more trivial way, of the Bruce character in the movie *Bruce Almighty*. Bruce thinks he's qualified to be God, so God allows him to give it a shot for a couple of days. In one scene, Bruce realizes that millions of prayers are being prayed at exactly the same moment, and when he attempts to answer them all, he collapses in hysteria. He simply can't do it. I saw myself as partnering with God — which is a biblical concept — but I had exaggerated *my* part of the partnership and quickly found that, like misguided Bruce, my shoulders were not broad enough to carry the weight of the world. I was caving in, being brought low to the ground by a burden beyond the scope of my ability to bear. Somehow I forgot that any pain I felt in response to the pain of another originated in the heart of God, not in mine. As a result, I was inadvertently cheating myself out of the consolation and comfort available to me through sharing in the *fellowship* of the sufferings of Jesus.

I had to surrender my desire to save the world.

As we sat in Pastor Mike's office and processed our experiences, I realized that my time with the prostitutes in Calcutta had allowed me to love them and to pray they would come to know Jesus through the way we loved them. But when I was sitting on the dusty floor of the tearoom, I had only been dimly aware that I could share *with Jesus* the pain I was feeling for the misery of the women. He didn't plan for me to carry their pain by myself, even though that was exactly what I was trying to do. I had felt God's love for these three women. I had felt his pain for their wounds. Now I was aware that as my heart continued to break for them, so did his. I knew that Jesus and I were united in our devotion to them. I sensed the oneness of sharing in his sufferings in a new way.

It was an unexpected bond.

A few months later, I was able to call on that bond of sharing in the fellowship of Jesus' sufferings during a visit to an orphanage for HIV-positive children in Kenya run by a dedicated elderly priest named Father Dag.

The high, clear voice of a young child caught my attention as Elizabeth and I walked the path between the cottages. Someone was singing — beautifully — in heavily accented English. Elizabeth and I were drawn to the voice. We had to see who was filling the air with such lovely sound. As we approached one cottage, the door wide open, we could see a young girl who looked to be about ten years old, sitting on the floor putting on her shoes. She didn't see us at first, and she continued with her song. Suddenly, we looked at each other

in amazement as we recognized the tune and the words —
and we fell mute with the poignancy of what we heard:

Somewhere over the rainbow
Bluebirds fly.
Birds fly over the rainbow.
*Why then, oh why can't I?**

We listened for a few moments and attempted to join in
her song, but trying to sing, "Birds fly over the rainbow, why
then, oh why can't I?" was impossible. Our voices faltered
and quit, choked by tears. By then she had seen us standing
in the doorway and was embarrassed that we had overheard
her, but she smiled at us and hugged us after she finished
tying her shoes. I'll never forget her. Where she learned that
old American song, I'll never know, but she articulated the
dearest hope of orphans everywhere — the wistful hope that
somewhere, someday, they will wake up where "clouds are
far behind," where "troubles melt like lemon drops," where
the sky is blue and dreams *will* come true — dreams of a
home, of a place to belong, of a family.

We continued through the cottages to the carefully
tended cemetery. Tiny mounds of dirt and small white
crosses marked the resting places of orphans infected by
HIV-positive mothers, most of whom never even knew they
were sick. "This is too much, Jesus," I cried. "Little ones
should be running, playing, jumping, getting into mischief,
laughing, growing, learning — not dying before they get
to live." In my grief for these babies whose lives were cut
short by HIV and for the girl with the beautiful voice who
may never find a home, I had to forcibly remind myself to

* Excerpt from "Over the Rainbow," lyrics by E. Y. Harburg.

draw on the comfort Jesus offered. Mine wasn't the only heart aching with the unfairness and pain of it all, with the waste of innocent life. Jesus wept too. He and Elizabeth and I shared a bond.

Jesus holds out to all of us the possibility of fellowship with him. He suffered *with us* and *for us*, and now we are privileged to suffer *with him*, *for him*, and *with those he loves*. But we all have spiritual ADD — we're easily distracted, forgetful, and absentminded. So he has provided a tangible reminder of his sufferings, a way in which we can experience this unbreakable bond with him.

He offers us his body and his blood.

PRIVATE PROFOUND COMMUNION

When I was growing up, our church observed the Lord's Supper every few months. It was always a solemn occasion, and each child was given strict instructions about how to behave during those few moments of eating a dry piece of unleavened cracker and drinking grape juice from a tiny plastic cup. I remember living in mortal fear that I would drop the cup held in my trembling fingers. I worried that I would eat the piece of unleavened bread at the wrong moment. Worst of all, I was scared to death that I would think unholy thoughts while holding this sacred reminder of Jesus' death for me. There were a couple of times when I got tickled about something and did my best to stifle the giggles, but there is something about trying not to laugh that just makes you laugh harder. I had two powerfully conflicting reactions: this is a holy moment and I need to be serious, and this is a hilarious moment and I can't stop laughing — God is going to strike me dead! Even as an adult I often found myself anxious when it came time to remember Jesus' sacrifice for my sins. Rarely did eating the bread and drinking the cup stir anything passionate in my soul.

This all began to change when I caught a glimpse of the fellowship with Christ that was available to me. From Scripture I knew that he and I were now united because of his death on the cross for my sins, but I can't say that I felt any power from this unity in my daily life. When I became aware that I could show my love for him by serving others, the realities of the dimension I cannot see, touch, taste, smell, or hear became concrete. The knowledge that I could offer Jesus a drink of water, clothe his nakedness, feed his hunger, relieve his loneliness, and stand with him in devotion by his cross through giving to someone else opened up a depth of intimacy that my soul had craved. It all became *real* to me. Eating the bread and drinking the juice that represent his body and blood became an experience in which I could delight in deep communion with Almighty God and in fellowship with the community of believers with whom I share my life. I love it that the Bible's word for *fellowship* — *koinonia* — is the same word used for *communion*. Fellowship. Communion. With him and with each other.

The apostle Paul makes this observation:

> When we ask the Lord's blessing upon our drinking from the cup of wine at the Lord's Table, this means, doesn't it, that all who drink it are sharing together the blessing of Christ's blood? And when we break off pieces of the bread from the loaf to eat there together, this shows that we are sharing together in the benefits

of his body. No matter how many of us there are, we all eat from the same loaf, showing that we are all parts of the one body of Christ.

1 Corinthians 10:16 – 17 LB

Communing with Christ through the bread and the cup — sharing in the fellowship of his sufferings — is the greatest privilege of a relationship with God. As Oswald Chambers declares, we now have "private profound communion with Him."[18] The second greatest privilege of a relationship with God is personal profound communion with each other. My favorite wisdom from Henri Nouwen is this:

> Nothing is sweet or easy about community. Community is a fellowship of people who do not hide their joys and sorrows but make them visible to each other in a gesture of hope. In community we say: "Life is full of gains and losses, joys and sorrows, ups and downs — but we do not have to live it alone. We want to drink our cup together and thus celebrate the truth that the wounds of our individual lives, which seem intolerable when lived alone, become sources of healing when we live them as part of a fellowship of mutual care."[19]

This fellowship of mutual care, of communion with each other, means that in the deepest sense possible we are truly never alone again — never alone in our pain, never alone in our joy, never alone in our shame, never alone in our success, never alone in our failure, never alone in our grief, never alone in our celebrations. We belong to a community!

In community, our misguided attempts to save the world by ourselves are challenged. In community, our motivations are held up to loving scrutiny. In community, the weight of the world is carried by other committed Christ-followers. In community, we go into his presence together to share the celebration of his sacrifice for our sins. In community, courageous surrender on the part of a group member is a cause for rejoicing, not a decision to ridicule and mock. We are united to Jesus Christ and to each other.

Jesus died to make "private profound communion" with God possible. It is this communion that makes all of the suffering we endure for ourselves and for others bearable. In his presence — in fellowship with him and with each other — we are restored, rebuilt, renewed, refreshed, and refitted for the public activity to which he calls us. But before the public activity comes the call to be with him in the fellowship of his sufferings, to enjoy this unexpected bond.

SURRENDER

Will you let your pain — and the suffering
of others you have chosen to bear —
draw you into intimate fellowship with Jesus?

Father, I want to know you and to be known by you. Forgive me for reducing a relationship with you to rules to follow, one more item to check off my daily to-do list. I am busy with public activity. I rush around most mornings like I've been shot out of a cannon. While I know you have work for me to do, I first want to commune with you on a level that defies human explanations. At times I find myself unwilling or unable to really share my life in rich communion with other believers. Please draw me into the fellowship of Jesus' sufferings so that I may share it with you and with those in my spiritual community. I'm so grateful for the Lord's Supper and the mystery it reveals and the power it imparts. May the knowledge that I am one with you through Jesus Christ guide my activities today.

Prayer

SAY YES TO GOD

○ Pause and consider this question: "Where have I attempted to carry the weight of the world on my shoulders?" If you have a reading partner, deepen your fellowship by sharing your insights. After you've had opportunity to think about your response to suffering, take time to read and reflect on this paraphrase of Jesus' words from the gospel of Matthew: "Are you tired? Worn out? Burned out on religion? Come to me. Get away with me and you'll recover your life. I'll show you how to take a real rest. Walk with me and work with me — watch how I do it. Learn the unforced rhythms of grace. I won't lay anything heavy or ill-fitting on you. Keep company with me and you'll learn to live freely and lightly" (Matthew 11:28 – 30 MSG).

○ The next time your church observes the Lord's Supper (Communion), approach it with a renewed tenderness and joy as you enter into intimacy with Jesus and your brothers and sisters in God's family.

○ Listen to the inspiring song "Carried to the Table" by Leeland (sung by Nikki Lalague). For a limited time, you will be able to hear it at www.kaywarren.com.

10

LINKING ARMS

*God has put all things under the authority of Christ
and has made him head over all things for the benefit
of the church. And the church is his body;
it is made full and complete by Christ,
who fills all things everywhere with himself.*

Ephesians 1:22–23 NLT

*The church is her true self only
when she exists for humanity.*

Dietrich Bonhoeffer, *Letters and Papers from Prison*

"I accepted Christ on the first night of the AIDS summit at Saddleback," the young man said between bites of pizza, "because I realized that the only hope for the world is the church. I've seen the efforts of people not connected with the church, and they just can't get the job done."

I was having lunch with some Saddleback staff members and this young man who had attended our annual Global Summit on AIDS and the Church. He is well connected in the film industry and had seen firsthand the sincere efforts of many who want to help with poverty, injustice, AIDS, and orphans. I had heard that he had gone back to his hotel room on the first night of the summit and made a commitment of his life to God, and I was curious to learn how our AIDS summit had drawn him to Christ — we hadn't even given an altar call!

He continued: "I sat in the middle of the crowd of people filling the auditorium and realized that *this* was the group of people who could actually make a difference — the church of Jesus Christ — and I suddenly knew this is where I wanted to be. I gave my life to Christ that day."

His story blows my mind. When was the last time you heard of someone who was so attracted by the beauty of Christ's church that they were compelled to become a part of it? I've grown accustomed to stories of people being repelled and angered by the church, so to hear of a man who saw the true worth of the church and was drawn to it was very moving to me. He was able to look beyond the flaws, failures, and foibles of the human beings who comprise Christ's church and see the vast potential God envisions — he saw the *hope*.

I confess that I spent a couple of years being seriously disturbed on behalf of people who suffer before I latched on to the hope. I had a very difficult time processing, filtering, and absorbing the new realities that I kept discovering, and even though I eventually learned how to join my suffering with the sufferings of Christ, I couldn't find much reason to be optimistic that the world's problems would change in any significant way.

I'm naturally a pessimistic person. In the "Winnie the Pooh school of personality types," I'm a classic Eeyore. I've struggled with depression most of my life, and I almost always see the glass as half empty. So for me to say honestly that I now have hope is a really big deal! It represents growth in my relationship with God and a greater understanding of and love for the source of my hope — his church.

Although I was raised in the church — enrolled in the Cradle Roll at the tender age of one week — my affection for Christ's church was largely one of duty. God planned the church from the beginning of time, Jesus died for the church, and the Holy Spirit empowers the church. I knew these truths from Scripture, but they weren't something I connected with on an emotional level.

I have witnessed through the years both the pain and the pleasure of being a part of the church. As a pastor's wife, I had been frustrated by infighting, territorialism, divisions, and schisms within the church at large. I found denominationalism a roadblock to believers working together to bring people to Christ. I was embarrassed by the "do what I say, not what I do" behavior of some Christians in the public square. The blind eye turned toward the physical needs of our brothers and sisters angered me. Like many others, I have felt like giving up and often contemplated alternative ways to get God's work done without involving the church.

God chose a graphic method to change my mind.

HOPE LOST — AND FOUND

After finishing my cancer treatments in the spring of 2004, I could hardly wait to travel again — to resume my God-given call to be an HIV/AIDS advocate for those who have no voice. The biennial International AIDS Conference was taking place in Bangkok, Thailand, in July 2004, and my friend Elizabeth, her teenage son, my teenage son, a young couple from our church, and I traveled to participate in the weeklong conference with thousands of others from around the world. We were shocked to enter the convention center and be confronted instantly with a large display chronicling a day in the life of a commercial sex worker (prostitute) — not in a negative way, but from the perspective that prostitution is good and that it is necessary in a society. From there, the shock waves continued. Red paint was thrown on a large poster of the president of the United States, and anti-American sentiments were expressed freely by speaker after speaker. It seemed as though every speaker began his or her talk with the phrase "We must consider the rights of gay, lesbian, bisexual, transgender people; commercial sex workers; and IV drug users." In the exhibit hall, a large remote-controlled condom floated over the attendees, while beautiful evening gowns crafted from dyed condoms that had been formed into a variety of shapes were on display. The ideas of saving sex for marriage and fidelity in marriage were ridiculed, rejected, and labeled ineffective in the fight against HIV transmission. It seemed as though every ideal and value I held on to was being turned upside down by the presenters — up was down, and down was up; right was wrong, and wrong was right; light was darkness, and darkness was light.

This perspective — a worldview, in fact — fully embraced by thousands in the convention center, was still brand-new to me, and I had a lot to process. I walked through the cavernous convention center with my mouth hanging open in shock and disbelief at the assault on my values, the promotion of sexual license, and the anti-Americanism I hadn't been exposed to before. My brain was in a whirl trying to decipher medical terminology and scientific jargon and research results, and over it all was a layer of sadness, knowing the reality that millions of men, women, and children were dying from this evil virus.

A spirit of hopelessness began to build in me as the days of the conference went by. What had I gotten myself into? Whatever made me think I could do anything significant about AIDS? The problem was too big; too many people were sick. How do we get lifesaving medication to those who need it the most? How can we stop this pandemic from decimating country after country? What will happen to all of the children left alone to care for themselves? How can we end the stigma and rejection that people with HIV experience? There is so much controversy over prevention methods — do I really want to jump into *that* discussion?

I sat by myself in my hotel room on the last day, discouraged, the wind knocked out of my sails — feeling foolish and naive, quite sure I was an idiot for thinking I could make a difference in a problem that spanned the globe. There was no hope for ending AIDS — nothing of significance I or anyone else could really do. In my despair, I picked up my friend's Bible and randomly opened it. My eyes fell on Acts 26, which details the apostle Paul's retelling of his conversion story to King Agrippa. Once more, God reached into my soul and reaffirmed his call to me:

> "One day on my way to Damascus, armed as always with papers from the high priests authorizing my action, right in the middle of the day a blaze of light, light outshining the sun, poured out of the sky on me and my companions. Oh, King, it was so bright! We fell flat on our faces. Then I heard a voice in Hebrew: 'Saul, Saul,

why are you out to get me? Why do you insist on going against the grain?'

"I said, 'Who are you, Master?'

"The voice answered, 'I am Jesus, the One you're hunting down like an animal. But now, up on your feet — I have a job for you. I've handpicked you to be a servant and witness to what's happened today, and to what I am going to show you.

" 'I'm sending you off to open the eyes of the outsiders so they can see the difference between dark and light, and choose light, see the difference between Satan and God, and choose God. I'm sending you off to present my offer of sins forgiven, and a place in the family, inviting them into the company of those who begin real living by believing in me.'

"What could I do, King Agrippa? I couldn't just walk away from a vision like that! I became an obedient believer on the spot. I started preaching this life-change — this radical turn to God and everything it meant in everyday life — right there in Damascus, went on to Jerusalem and the surrounding countryside, and from there to the whole world."

Acts 26:12 – 20 MSG

In this impassioned appeal to King Agrippa, Paul is clearly overjoyed by the vision God has given him and declares that it would be impossible for him to walk away from such a vision. In that hotel room, I jumped up in excitement, and with tears falling down my cheeks, I lifted my arms to God and said, "God, I am yours! I see that I am to use whatever time you give me to call the church of Jesus Christ to repentance and action on behalf of those with HIV/AIDS, to be a voice for those who have no voice, to speak to those with all the power on behalf of those who have no power, and to encourage the church to make room in their hearts for the millions of children left vulnerable because of the death of their parents."

God's Word banished any remaining questions about what I was supposed to be doing with my life. There was no more doubt, no second-guessing; no ambivalence remained! God reminded me that he wants to use me to help point out the difference between dark and light so that many will choose *light*. He wants people to see the difference between Satan and God, and choose God. He asked me to tell those I meet that their sins are forgiven and that their search for a "home" and a family can come to an end — God wants them in *his* home. He reminded me to tell them that real living comes in relationship to him.

To this day, that reaffirmation of God's call on my life has not left me; I am living out my God-given purposes to the best of my ability. I live with intensity, passion, and drive. The goal is crystal clear now: end HIV/AIDS.

The only problem is that it's impossible.

With massive amounts of money, cooperation, coordination, and effort, we can slow down the spread of HIV — but end it? Not likely. Governments have tried and will continue to try to stop HIV/AIDS; corporations, big business, and philanthropists have tried and will keep on trying. The medical community has put forth a valiant effort to end AIDS but has yet to eradicate the virus. So why do I even have it as a goal? Because I believe that when the missing link — the church of Jesus Christ — rises from its slumber, awakens to the magnitude of the problem, acknowledges its sinful absence or puny

SAY YES TO GOD

efforts (at least in the West), repents of neglecting those God is passionate about, and rallies its best attention, effort, and compassion, HIV/AIDS can become a disease that *used* to plague our world.

If one International AIDS Conference left me hopeless, depressed, and convinced there was nothing any of us could really do, the next one left me excited, jubilant, and encouraged. Whereas I walked through the convention center in Bangkok in July 2004 with my head drooped in despair, my head was held high and there was a smile on my face in Toronto in August 2006. Why? Not much had changed in the world — millions are still infected with HIV, millions have died, millions of children are orphaned, the number of new infections is rising, there's no cure in sight, there's no vaccine to prevent infections. What in the world was there to be so happy about?

I had fallen in love with the church!

THE ONLY HOPE

I know it sounds crazy, but the church — with all its warts and flaws — has advantages over every other institution in society. More than two billion people claim to be followers of Jesus Christ — and this means that no organization is bigger than the church. No government, no relief agency — no single country, in fact — is bigger than the church. These churches are scattered in nearly every country on earth, and there are more churches than all of the McDonald's, Wal-Marts, Starbucks, and Macy's combined. Some places have a few or no hospitals or universities or libraries, but they have a church! Let's take a look at Rwanda as an example.

In Rwanda's West Province, there are three area hospitals.

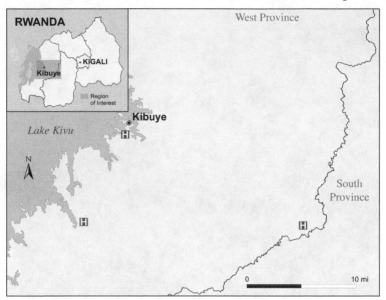

Figure 1: Rwanda, West Province: Hospitals (3)

Notice how the medical coverage is expanded through approximately twenty area health centers.

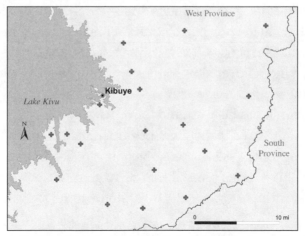

Figure 2: Rwanda, West Province: Health Centers (19)

Now see the vast penetration represented by more than seven hundred churches.

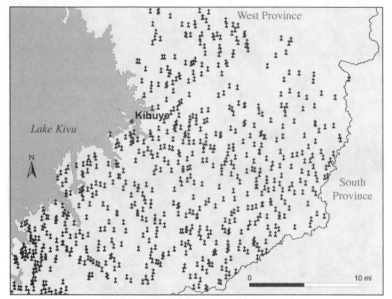

Figure 3: Rwanda, West Province: Churches (728)*

Churches are part of a grassroots networking system, which means they are much more efficient and effective than bureaucracies. The church around the world is growing at the rate of 60,000 new converts a day. To stop the HIV/AIDS pandemic requires something growing faster than the 7,000 new infections every day — and the church fits the bill. The church has been around for nearly two thousand years; it certainly isn't a fly-by-night operation. It has a track record of caring for the sick, helping the poor, and leading people to Jesus Christ. Jesus himself told us to go into the world and do his work (Matthew 28:19 – 20; John 17:18) — there is no

---

* *Kibuye, Rwanda.* Saddleback Church. December 2006. Information from National Institute of Statistics of Rwanda.

stronger authorization than that. The church offers love as the motivation for everything we do; the highest call on our lives is to love as Jesus loved (John 15:12 – 13). Governments and the private sector cannot love in the name of Jesus; only Christians can do that.

With many years of international travel as an HIV/AIDS advocate now under my belt, I've discovered through my interactions with leaders in numerous countries that, although many government employees are good people, lasting hope isn't found in governments. I've also had the opportunity to interact with some of the most influential businessmen and businesswomen, and again, though many are sharp, quality folks, hope isn't found in the private sector. Hope for sustainable, lasting societal change is found primarily in the church of Jesus Christ. Governments, regimes, empires, politicians, and policies come and go; in the overall scheme of things, none hang around for long. Businesses expand, recede, prosper, decline, and change direction and focus; there's little stability to count on over the long haul. But the church of Jesus is unique — and it holds out the only concrete possibility of change in individuals and in societies.

I'm cognizant of the enormity of what I'm saying. I'm painfully aware of the sins of those in the church throughout the ages — the injustice and evil, crimes, rapes, wars, theft, lying, and suffering perpetrated in God's name. I could talk for days about the sins and weaknesses of my fellow evangelicals that I've heard about in just the last few years. I'm even more aware of my own failures as a person who claims to be a Christ-follower. How else can I explain my absence from the fight against AIDS for the first twenty years? Truth be told, we're a pretty sorry lot. If you took an inventory, you'd be hard-pressed to find a completely whole and healthy person in the whole bunch. So why would I put any faith at all in such a ragtag bunch of losers?

Because God does.

As strange as it sounds, God has put all of his "eggs" in one basket, namely, his church. He has no other basket! His strategy has always been to work through his people — first he reminded the people of Israel that they had been blessed to be a blessing to others and gave them specific instructions on how to care for those made vulnerable by poverty, sickness, and injustice (Exodus 22:22; 23:11; Leviticus 19:15; Deuteronomy 24:17 – 19). Jesus clearly instructed his followers to do as he did — such things as preaching, teaching, and healing (Matthew 10:8; 25:35 – 45; Luke 9:2; 12:33). The writings of Paul and James further define what the church was established to be and do:

> Share with God's people who need help. Bring strangers in need into your homes.
>
> *Romans 12:13 NCV*

> Tell them to use their money to do good. They should be rich in good works and generous to those in need, always being ready to share with others.
>
> *1 Timothy 6:18 NLT*

> Religion that God our Father accepts as pure and faultless is this: to look after orphans and widows in their distress and to keep oneself from being polluted by the world.
>
> *James 1:27*

Throughout the centuries, the church has been at the forefront of caring for people in a holistic manner, addressing the needs of both body and soul.

Rick and I visited Nottingham Castle in Nottingham, England, a few years ago. In the basement of this immense and still regal castle, we saw a diorama that depicted life in the Middle Ages. We were thrilled to discover one scene of a cathedral in the center of town where the lame, the poor, and those in need were entering. Written next to the reenactment were these words: "The church influenced life from the cradle to the grave. Most holidays were religious festivals. Parish churches were the natural focus for the life of the community. The size of the church buildings meant they were used for public meetings. The church also helped the poor and provided education and hospitals."

What I'm suggesting is not new! A thousand years ago, this is what the church was known for, and it is what we should be known for today. God has commissioned those in his eternal family to be his hands and feet in the world, to be his voice of love, to speak truth, to act justly, to combat evil, and to do good. Our job is to push back the encroaching darkness and be God's light in a desperately dark world. Our mission is to care for the sick, the widows, the orphans — and to heal in Jesus' name. We are to preach the Good News of salvation and to disciple the nations, bringing all into fellowship with him and each other. The Lord of all calls us to live lives of love, mercy, and grace, thus making the invisible God visible. It's not a matter of one or the other; we must care for both body and soul. We are Christ's ambassadors. If we fail, he has no plan B.

With eyes wide open to the inconsistencies, mistakes, and even sins of all of us who are a part of Christ's church,

I still embrace his church with my whole heart. Where else would I go? What other family, home, or country will last into eternity? None but his church. What other institution has the power of Almighty God associated with it? None but his church. What other purposes besides his have the power to inspire men, women, and children to sacrifice all that they have so that others might find healing, help, and salvation? There are none. Nothing is more beautiful than the body of Christ — each believer connected to him and to each other, living out his purposes in their corner of the world.

In J. R. R. Tolkien's *The Return of the King*, the tiny little hobbits link their arms with each other and face their destiny. They don't go alone into the heat of the battle. This picture of friends joining their hearts, their allegiances, and their skills in pursuit of a common purpose captures the essence of the nature of our call. We don't go it alone. God has given us each other in a forever family called his church so that we do not face life by ourselves. We don't tackle impossible situations on our own. We never have to worry that when we answer his call, we will be stranded without a support system to back us up. We don't go after global Goliaths armed only with our personal slingshot. We move as a pack, as soldiers in the same battalion, as teammates playing for the same team, as musicians in the same band, as birds in the same flock, as brothers and sisters in the same family.

In the church of Jesus Christ, both the strong and the weak are needed. In a pack of animals, not every animal is of equal strength or ability. Every soldier in a battalion isn't equally fit or able to fight. Teammates often have widely varying skill levels. Orchestras have a "first chair" for several instruments because musical talent and experience vary. In a flock of birds, the strongest bird leads the weaker ones. Everybody knows that brothers and sisters are a motley conglomeration of talents, looks, gifts, strengths, and weaknesses. Typically, the youngest and the oldest members are the most at risk of harm or injury. But in every illustration, it is the responsibility of the strong to value and protect the weak and more vulnerable members and to ensure that the weakest ones cannot be lost.

In fact, Dietrich Bonhoeffer, the Lutheran pastor martyred by Adolf Hitler, goes so far as to draw this bold conclusion:

> In a Christian community everything depends upon whether every individual is an indispensable link in a chain. Only when even the smallest link is securely interlocked is the chain unbreakable.... Every Christian community must realize that not only do the weak need the strong, but also that the strong cannot exist without the weak. The elimination of the weak is the death of fellowship.[20]

Without God and his church, very little lasting change is possible. With God and his church, almost everything is possible. Will you link arms with me and millions of others — the weak and the strong — and commit to fighting spiritual lostness, corrupt leadership, extreme poverty, pandemic disease, and crippling illiteracy through local churches? Bonhoeffer spoke powerful truth when he declared, "The church is her true self only when she exists for humanity."[21] Will you join the greatest force for change on our planet?

SURRENDER

Will you commit to playing your part
in the body of Christ, his church,
as the hope of the world?

Father, I admit I haven't always been an
enthusiastic supporter of your church; in fact,
I've frequently been embarrassed by the public
failures and goofy statements of those who claim
to represent you. Up to this point, I haven't
been open to seeing the potential for the societal
and personal change that can happen if I and
other believers in Jesus Christ link arms and
determine to fight the global Goliaths through
local churches. I have put my hope for change
in temporary institutions that will not last
instead of in your church, which will continue
into eternity. I want to be a part of changing my
world starting today. Please use me in any way
you see fit.

SAY YES TO GOD

○ Become a positive advocate for your own local church by speaking well of it, in spite of its limitations. If you have a reading partner, discuss together various ways to mobilize your church for action.

○ What are some of the negative views of the church that many in our society hold? Is there any truth to the claims? If so, what do you think the church needs to do to change this impression?

○ Watch Kay's message "The Hope of the World" at www .kaywarren.com.

WHAT ARE YOU WILLING TO DIE FOR?

*"Do not be afraid of those who kill the body
but cannot kill the soul.
Rather, be afraid of the One who can destroy
both soul and body in hell."*

Matthew 10:28

*He is no fool who gives what he cannot keep
to gain that which he cannot lose.*

Jim Elliot, *The Journals of Jim Elliot*

THE EARLY-MORNING QUIET WAS SO PEACEFUL NOT EVEN the seagulls were awake yet. Rick and I were on vacation and going about the day in a no-rush way. We sat side by side on the porch, reading the morning news on our laptops. "Oh, Rick," I exclaimed, "three American missionaries were killed this morning in Yemen!" I didn't know these missionaries, but their deaths hit me hard; it felt very personal. The Polaroid picture of God's will for me was growing sharper by the day, and I was in the planning stages of my first trip to Africa. Hearing of their murders on December 30, 2002, brought home the fact that the stakes are high. Was I willing to sacrifice as much as they had for Jesus' sake? I grabbed my journal.

*News this morning of three Southern Baptist missionary
doctors shot to death in Yemen. My mind is a blur of
thoughts and emotions, mostly sadness for their families,
for the pain of losing loved ones in such a brutal manner.
In an odd way, they were blessed with a quick death — no
torture, no abuse, no drawn-out wait for their release, no
suffering, just instant transport into the Father's presence!
In that sense, there can be joy. Isn't that our ultimate goal
anyway — to meet him face-to-face? It was a surprise.
None of them got up in the morning and said, "I'm going
to die today" — so it must have come as a shock to realize
their final moments on earth were coming to a close.
But these doctors were serving in one of the most hostile
environments, a place where Americans and Christians
are hated. They knowingly served at great personal risk
and must have counted the cost over and over, deciding
that the call was worth the cost. I admire their sacrificial
offering of their very lives to God — echoing Queen Esther,
who said, "If I perish, I perish." They not only professed
their willingness to give all they had for the sake of the
gospel; they lived it.*

*Father, as I meditate on what you have for me in
the coming years, I, too, am willing to give up my life if
it brings your lost children back to you. If by my death
the "Jesus way" becomes clearer in the minds of those
confused by the claims of false gods, then my life is yours.*

There is a cost to surrendering to God — to saying yes
unequivocally with no reservations, no strings attached, no
escape clauses. Being willing to say "whatever it takes" — and
mean it — is dangerous. At the very least, surrendering yourself to "whatever it takes" means dying to self and selfish

ambition, and at the most extreme, it may mean giving up your very life. For most of us, dying for Jesus' sake is not something we will be asked to do, but in the deepest places in our souls, we must come to the place where we are *willing* to die if it serves God's purposes.

I've heard it said my whole life: the safest place in the world is in the center of God's will. I understand the spirit of those words, and you probably do as well, but I wonder if we've ever recognized that it is also the most dangerous place to be. As Jesus prayed in the garden of Gethsemane before Judas betrayed him, the Savior's anguished yes to God demonstrated that he knew *exactly* the implications of his courageous surrender. Jesus was in the center of God's will when it led him to the cross of execution.

It is possible to live a "safe" life as a Christian — never really developing a rugged faith that is willing to take risks for Jesus' sake — but living in a protective bubble won't change the world. As Dietrich Bonhoeffer said, "When Christ calls [us], he bids [us] come and die."[22]

My first trip to Africa in March 2003 — to Mozambique — was on the eve of the war in Iraq. The United States was abuzz with talk of war and troops being deployed, and the level of terror risk was rated at red — the highest level. I debated back and forth in my mind whether to postpone the trip. I don't like to fly in the best of circumstances, and flying to a place so far away with the specter of September 11, 2001, still fresh in my mind gave me plenty of reasons to be nervous and anxious. Rick was supportive, but the rest of my family members and friends were very worried for my safety. In the end, it was the words of Queen Esther — "If I perish, I perish" (Esther 4:16) — that helped me decide. Her reckless abandonment to God's will gave me the courage to take the trip as planned.

When I woke up that first morning in Mozambique, two-inch headlines in the newspaper confirmed that the United States was at war. I felt vulnerable anyway, but I was conscious that I was separated from my family, my home, and my country at a precarious moment in history. It was a sacrifice I had become willing to make, and it allowed me to expand my trust in God's care for me, even in a possibly dangerous situation.

Dangerous surrender is exactly that — *dangerous.*

DISCIPLINE, SACRIFICE, COST

We are such wimps — really, we are. Living in a sophisticated developed country where life is full of comfort and conveniences has weakened our character and our resolve. We often look for the easy way out of challenging situations and even pride ourselves on doing the minimum required — just enough to get by. Discipline, sacrifice, cost — these are not popular concepts.

When was the last time you read a magazine article on how to grow in self-sacrifice? About the only time we're willing to be self-disciplined or self-sacrificing or to pay a price is when it has a personal benefit to ourselves — when it helps us achieve a goal that matters to us. We keep hoping we can get something for nothing. We cling to the fantasy that following Jesus won't cost us anything.

Not so!

Remember the great examples of courageously surrendered heroes of the faith in the letter to the Hebrews?

I could go on and on, but I've run out of time. There are so many more — Gideon, Barak, Samson, Jephthah, David, Samuel, the prophets.... Through acts of faith, they toppled kingdoms, made justice work, took the promises for themselves. They were protected from lions, fires, and sword thrusts, turned disadvantage to advantage, won battles, routed alien armies. Women received their loved ones back from the dead. There were those who, under torture, refused to give in and go free, preferring something better: resurrection. Others braved abuse and whips, and, yes, chains and dungeons. We have stories of those who were stoned, sawed in two, murdered in cold blood; stories of vagrants wandering the earth in animal skins, homeless, friendless, powerless — the world didn't deserve them! — making their way as best they could on the cruel edges of the world.

Not one of these people, even though their lives of faith were exemplary, got their hands on what was promised. God had a better plan for us: that their faith and our faith would come together to make one completed whole, their lives of faith not complete apart from ours.

Hebrews 11:32–40 MSG

The courageous folks mentioned in this passage were attacked by lions, tortured, mocked, whipped, chained in dungeons, stoned to death, sawed in half, pierced with swords, forced to go hungry, oppressed, and mistreated. Many were wanderers with no permanent home, often resorting to hiding in caves or holes in the ground. Through the centuries, others like them have preferred torture and death to betraying Jesus. Their kind is still around. Three modern-day martyrs were horribly mutilated before being killed in Turkey recently simply because they had chosen Jesus as their Savior. Following Jesus does not come without a price tag.

Most of us shudder with fear when we hear the stories of those martyred for their faith; I know I do. The truth is that God doesn't ask most of us to pay that price. Most of us are called to pay a much smaller price, although each point of surrender can at times turn into high drama as we play tug-of-war with God: "No, God, don't ask me to surrender that. I can't. I don't want to. Please don't ask for *that*." Often as we keep praying, as we keep seeking, we know for certain that in order to remain in an intimate conversation with him, *that* very thing is what we need to yield.

Sometimes we must yield something as ordinary or common as our personal relationships. I have to be honest — surrendering all that we are to God does not always lead to peaceful relationships. At first, my children were tolerant of my forays into the world of advocating for people with HIV because they loved me and wanted me to do what I felt called to do. They themselves are generous, compassionate young adults. But before long, tension and conflict surfaced.

Throughout our children's growing-up years, our family chose to live a simpler lifestyle so I could be at home with them. For a while, I did child care in my home, and at one point I even did some ironing jobs for other people so I wouldn't have to work outside of our home. I was very involved in Saddleback Church's ministry but always stayed available for the kids, even after they became adults. Now, at this new stage of life, my suddenly expanding world and my emerging role as an HIV/AIDS advocate came as a shock to all of us.

My life morphed before our eyes. It began with just caring about people with HIV/AIDS. As that ministry increased, I began working out of my home office but quickly moved to an office building. In the beginning I worked part-time, but within months I was working full-time for the first time in twenty-five years. Soon I was traveling internationally and became less involved in the day-to-day ministry of our church. Rick had always told me that someday God would use me in ways I couldn't imagine, but when it started to happen, the changes created a lot of discomfort for all of us. I was no longer the same person. There were times when my children felt as though they didn't know me anymore.

It has been a painful time for everyone. We have spent hours and hours sharing with each other and listening to each other's fears, concerns, worries, and even grief. My precious daughter, Amy, was at the stage of life when she was having children, and she wanted me around to share in these experiences on a daily basis. She was used to my being readily available. One day she poured out her heart and said, "I miss you, Mom. I see other grandmothers going to the park with their grandkids every week — they're available to go to lunch with their daughters at a moment's notice, they go shopping together, they hang out, and I wanted that for us. I have to let go of my expectations of you, and it hurts."

Just typing these words makes me cry. I *adore* my children and grandchildren so deeply that it actually aches. Who wouldn't want to spend enormous amounts of time with your grown children and grandkids, especially if they *want* to be with you? My kids are some of my best friends.

My grandbabies touch a visceral place in me, and my love for them is fierce.

At the same time …

The reality of the motherless and fatherless children of our world also pierces my heart. I think of how tragic it would have been if my three kids had grown up without parents. When I fix lunch for my grandchildren, I can't help but hurt for the millions of children who scrounge through garbage dumps for edible crumbs. As I cuddle with Kaylie, Cassidy, Caleb, or Cole as they drift off to sleep, I hear in my mind's eye the frantic cries of babies abandoned on the side of the road or in a field. I feel the despair and hopelessness of children wandering on the streets of the world's cities. I see the faces of abused little girls rescued from evil child prostitution. I can still feel the warmth of orphaned three-year-old Nisende's body nestled close to mine. All I want is for the world's children to have what my beloved grandbabies have. So I must ask myself, "If *I* don't speak for them, who will? If *I* don't mother them, who will?" Surely God can enable us to care for both our own families and those who have no family.

The faces of HIV-positive men and women I've met rouse me from sleep night after night. I recall the wasted body of Joanna under the tree. I wince as I hear Flora's poignant question, "Who will care for my children when I die?" I think of Alberto in Santa Ana, California, who had AIDS and lived in the backyard of a relative because of it. I feel Don's vulnerability as he expressed his hope that he wouldn't die alone. I remember the Global Summit on AIDS and the Church where I held the shaking body of Barb, an HIV-positive friend, as she wept with joy, knowing that Christians had accepted her. I can see the light dawning in the eyes of my AIDS activist friend David as he experienced the love of Jesus Christ for the first time.

These are the people who have changed me forever. They are the ones who have propelled me into moving beyond my comfortable life to embrace a more dangerous one. It's a life not without joy and pleasure — but it's a life that can no longer hope that someone else will answer God's call to care. I'm not the same person I was eight years ago; my life truly reads like a "before" and "after" story.

THE "AFTER" LIFE

Not much from my "before" life remains. I don't have as much time now to keep my house orderly or to cook wonderful meals for my husband and our young adult son who is still at home. We often have nothing but boxes of mac and cheese and bananas in the house — or a bunch of Weight Watchers dinners in the freezer. Laundry stacks up — but it's just my own, because Rick and Matthew now do their own. I couldn't have lived this way in an earlier season of life — you can't raise kids with absent parents, empty cupboards, and dirty underwear! I have pretty much stopped reading the newspaper, though I skim numerous magazines and do some perusing of news online.

Rick and I have to be very intentional about our relationship; our busy lives could easily take us in separate directions (and have on occasion), resulting in a decrease in our sense of intimacy with each other. We have to be deliberate in setting aside time for each other. I have to be more deliberate in all of my relationships — children, parents, siblings, and friendships. Time that used to be spent with my girlfriends now is given to business and ministry relationships. Some of my girlfriends have been disappointed by my inability to do friendship in the way I did previously; it hurts me as well because I love them. My commitment to my small group of three other couples who have helped me walk through my transformation remains strong. While my overall relationship time has lessened, I am more willing than ever to have our small group speak truth into my life and hold me accountable for personal growth and maturity.

Our congregation and church staff members have had to adjust to my very visible role in promoting the PEACE Plan and the HIV/AIDS ministry. As Saddleback grew over the years, I led the women's ministry and served in the new members' ministry, the college ministry, and finally in our ministry to our pastors' wives. In each instance, God eventually led me to give that ministry away to others. Now my focus is much narrower as my energies point like a laser beam toward eradicating HIV/AIDS.

I have limited the places to which I will travel and speak. Unless the event planners want me to talk about HIV/AIDS and the role of the church or about calling men and women to caring holistically for people, I usually don't accept their invitation.

My voice has gotten stronger. I am more comfortable using my prophetic gifts that call people to repentance and transformation. Doing so has led to my being a target of public scrutiny and criticism. Through the years as Rick's wife, I seldom received any personal criticism from outsiders. Saddleback Church and Rick have taken personal hits from the very beginning, but they were only mine at arm's length. Much of the criticism about the church was painful to me, but it wasn't about *me*.

Now I am a target personally. I've had to grow thicker skin while allowing my heart to grow softer. There are people on both sides of HIV advocacy who dislike me. Some who are ideologically on the "far right" find my attempts unbiblical and misguided; others think I'm a kindhearted fool. Some on the "far left" find me homophobic and ignorant and view my efforts as unwelcome. One wounded person even wrote me an email containing these cruel words: "I wish you had died of breast cancer." Stabbing, shocking words — but no worse than the ugly experiences of gay men and women who have heard the taunt "Die, fag!" through the years, mostly from the lips of Christians. Suddenly I'm on the receiving end of the vicious words that sting. For someone who has always been extra-sensitive to criticism, this has been painful and a place of necessary growth in maturity and toughness. I can't worry about what other people think of me anymore. If I do, I'll be crippled.

GREAT GAINS

Yes, there is a cost associated with dangerous surrender, but there have also been gains — positive gains that have deepened my character, sharpened my skills, and emboldened my faith. I have faced fears of public speaking and the decades-old habit of comparing my gifts to Rick's gifts. I am more flexible and relaxed about what I need in advance about everything — plans, details, information about speaking, how I'm doing it. I am growing in my comfort level in social settings. I am astonished that the introverted geek who always sought the potted palm tree in the corner and one person to talk with the whole evening now talks to prominent people with more ease than I ever imagined possible.

Dangerous surrender has meant I have significantly fewer fears about germs or getting sick as I touch and hold sick people. I fly everywhere, even with less discomfort when I'm on smaller planes. I am willing to take more risks in every domain of my life. Whether the issue is physical safety, emotional vulnerability, or spiritual exploration of the tough questions of life, I am more willing to trust God. I am more willing to believe God for miracles, to surrender control, and to live with ambiguity and uncertainty. I am more comfortable with mystery and unanswered questions, more trusting of God's sovereignty, more dependent on God for strength than ever before yet also more confident in my own abilities and gifts. I am more willing to see new points of view and examine life through a different grid. I am far more passionate about making my life count. I've gained a sense of partnership with Almighty God — an intimacy with him that I've longed for — and I know that my heart beats with his like never before. These are the benefits of dangerous surrender.

Is it worth the sacrifices? Would I do it again? Yes — oh yes. But has it come with a cost? More than I could have imagined. Is the cause worth the cost? YES. At the end of the day, I'm not an advocate for people with HIV merely for their sakes; I do what I do for Jesus' sake. Because I am his and he is mine, I long to surrender myself to him. I long to be what he wants me to be — to love as he loves, to be broken by the things that break his heart, to be his hands and feet in the world. I long to pour myself out on behalf of those who are hurting — although not just for them. I do it as a way of loving Jesus. Jesus loves them, and so I will love them. He is my first love.

In this process of letting go of the life I knew and was comfortable with and taking hold of a new life that was unknown and uncomfortable, God has made my life a miracle. The young girl and woman who was terrified that she would only ever be ordinary and average has seen God multiply the small "lunch" yielded to him with trembling hands into bread that feeds others. He has done what he promised. The ordinary is transformed into extraordinary and the mundane into miraculous when surrendered to the Master. He is making of my life — and the lives of those whose stories I've told — "bread and wine" that can provide nourishment and hope for spiritually hungry and thirsty souls.

I have nothing in myself to offer — but Christ *in* me does. He has made my life a sacramental offering through the wounds I've received in my life — molestation, secret sinful behavior that I couldn't control, marital conflict, two bouts with cancer, and other wounds known only to him. God's way of preparing me to be an advocate for people with HIV has involved a painful journey, and I've protested more times than I can count that I'm not up to the task. I've wrongly accused him of being uncaring and unfeeling toward me. And yet without the wounding, I would not be the person I am today. There would be no "bread" or "wine" to offer to someone else without God's crushing fingers.

Just when I think I can't keep on going for one more minute, God provides other travelers along the road to encourage me and give me a swift kick in the pants. François Fénelon, Jim and Elisabeth Elliot, Amy Carmichael, Henri Nouwen, Oswald Chambers, and many others — their surrendered lives have nourished my soul and strengthened my resolve. These words from Chambers summarize so well God's call on our lives:

> We make calls out of our own spiritual consecration, but when we get right with God He brushes all these aside, and rivets us with a pain that is terrific to one thing we never dreamed of, and for one radiant flashing moment we see what He is after, and we say — "Here am I, send me."
>
> This call has nothing to do with personal sanctification but with being made broken bread and poured-out wine. God can never make us wine if we object to the fingers He uses to crush us with. If God would only use His own fingers, and make me broken bread and poured-out wine in a special way! But when He uses someone whom we dislike, or some set of circumstances to which we said we would never submit, and makes those the crushers, we object. We must never choose the scene of our own martyrdom. If ever we are going to be made into wine, we will have to be crushed; you cannot drink grapes. Grapes become wine only when they have been squeezed.
>
> I wonder what kind of finger and thumb God has been using to squeeze you, and you have been like a marble and escaped? You are not ripe yet, and if God *had* squeezed you, the wine would have been remarkably bitter. To be a sacramental personality means that the elements of the natural life are presenced by God as they are broken providentially in His service. We have to be adjusted into God before we can be broken bread in His hands. Keep right with God and let Him do what

He likes, and you will find that He is producing the kind of bread and wine that will benefit His other children.[23]

What a marvelous picture! My life, in God's fingers, can become bread and wine that offers sustenance to others on their journey. Too often I am like the person Chambers describes — squirming out from under God's fingers to avoid being crushed and thus missing out on being made into the bread and wine that feed another. Wheat cannot be made into bread without the threshing floor. Grapes will never yield their sweetness without the winepress. Do you see yourself in this description? How have you been avoiding God's hands? Is the cause worth the cost to you?

THE CAUSE IS WORTH THE COST

I'm a girlie girl when it comes to movies — no science fiction, fantasy, or war movies for me — but as I've told you, somehow the metaphorical world created in the Lord of the Rings trilogy has become a favorite. I am enthralled by the story of ordinary — in fact, rather silly — little hobbits, who are swept up into the ultimate battle between good and evil and the promised return of the king. My heart beats raggedly as the Ringwraiths gallop closer and closer to the elf princess Arwen as she valiantly tries to outrace them, holding the wounded Frodo in her arms. I smile at the antics of Merry and Pippin and take delight in watching them mature from ditzy, happy-go-lucky young men into seasoned fighters. Gollum's tortured soul reminds me of the never-ending conflict within myself as I vacillate between right and wrong. I resonate with the tender friendship that develops between

Sam and Frodo, and Sam's sacrificial giving of himself on behalf of Frodo vividly encourages me to serve my friends with that same intense loyalty.

The growing power of evil builds quickly, and before long, all that is good in the world is threatened by Saruman and his grotesque army of Orcs. In the third movie, *The Return of the King*, Aragorn, Gandolf the wizard, hobbits, and forces from the elves, the world of men, dwarves, and others stand still, eyeing the forces of Saruman. Saruman has created evil giants — Uruk-hai — by crossing Orcs and men. The forces of good take stock of themselves and their enemies and realize that they are vastly outnumbered — in both manpower and weaponry. Aragorn searches the faces of his beloved companions; the grim set of their jaws reveals their understanding that many of them will die in this ferocious clash. With his sword raised high above his head, Aragorn turns toward the amassed army of evil, lets out a thunderous roar of defiance, and begins running toward the forces of darkness. His comrades rally to his battle cry and plunge head-on into what will very likely be their doom. Bodies fly every which way; knives, swords, and hatchets hack off limbs and heads — and before long, the battlefield is strewn with the dying and the dead.

Wonder of wonders, the forces of good prevail! Weakness triumphs over strength in an unexpected victory. The hobbits, elves, and men could never have foreseen their outnumbered troops beating back the enemy, which made their willingness to sacrifice themselves even nobler. What made them fling themselves into battle against a stronger army, knowing they would most likely die in the effort? Why were they willing to risk being mortally wounded? They believed that the cause was worth the cost. They believed that their efforts — including the possibility that they would die — might usher in the return of their king.

Following my third dose of chemo, I left the hospital discouraged and disheartened. My blood counts as well as my spirits were low. I was vulnerable to picking up an infection from being around other people. However, I was so tired of being isolated and removed from daily life that Rick proposed we go to a matinee where fewer people would likely attend. He wanted to see *The Return of the King* — not exactly my first choice since I was feeling so depressed — but I was too drained to come up with an alternate suggestion. So a few days before Christmas, I wearily plopped into the theater seat. Before long, I was caught up in the powerful drama unfolding on the screen. I wept as Sam pledged to carry Frodo the last steps of their journey up Mount Doom. His tender declaration "I can't carry the Ring, Mr. Frodo, but I can carry you" reminded me of my family and friends who were carrying me through cancer. I wept even more as the brave soldiers fought their way through the layers of the evil army. They exuded unbelievable strength and courage as they committed to holding nothing back.

Throughout my cancer treatments, many people commended me for being strong and brave. Sitting in that dark theater, I knew I was neither brave nor strong; in fact, just the opposite was true. I admit to being scared to death most of the time. But through the medium of a movie — a story of ordinary characters who rise to an enormous challenge and become disciplined and sacrificial — I discovered a story that became a metaphor for my life. I caught a vision again of why I'm doing what I'm doing and why dangerous surrender is required. These movie characters were willing to sacrifice their agendas and plans to fight a battle against evil; I am too. They were willing to lay down their lives for their friends; I am too. They were willing to surrender everything dear to them if it might hasten the return of their king; I am too. I don't know when Jesus Christ is coming back, but he is my King. I will serve him in any way he asks me to in order to hasten his return; he's the only one who can — once and for all — fix what is broken in our torn-up world.

The cost is high — higher than we anticipate. But surrendering our lives to him and being willing to pay the highest price open up the certainty that justice will finally roll down like a river — that every tear will be wiped away, mercy will triumph over judgment, orphans will have families, these fragile bodies that get sick will know health, and love will win!

The call is *definitely* worth the cost.

I concluded my journal entry on December 30, 2002 — the day three Christians were martyred for their faith — with these words written by John Baillie as a morning prayer for the twenty-seventh day of each month:

> *For the power of His cross in the history of the world since He came:*
>> *For all who have taken up their own crosses and have followed Him:*
>> *For the noble army of martyrs and for all who are willing to die that others might live:*
>> *For all suffering freely chosen for noble ends, for pain bravely endured, for temporal sorrows that have been used for the building up of eternal joys:*
>>> *I praise and bless Thy holy name.*[24]

Are you willing to become disturbed? Are you willing to become ruined? Are you willing to make a courageous surrender? Will you expose and oppose evil wherever you find it? Will you join the battle? Will you make the invisible God visible by being his hands and feet in this broken world — by doing good? Will you link arms with me and millions of others who are committed to pursuing the global Goliaths through the local church? Will you offer yourself to God's loving fingers to become broken bread and poured-out wine that can minister life to spiritually starving, thirsty souls? Are you willing to risk it all for his sake? Will you say yes to God?

If so, your world is waiting ...

SURRENDER

Will you risk your life and all you hold dear
for the sake of God's kingdom?

Prayer

God, I'm not sure that I'm strong enough,
courageous enough, or disciplined enough to pay
the necessary price to see your kingdom come. I
have gotten lazy, usually looking for a way out of
difficulty rather than facing it head-on. Would
you remind me today that the cause is worth any
cost I might have to pay? I'm willing to believe
that you are a rewarder of those who seek you,
and I can anticipate that while I may be asked to
give up something precious to me, I will also gain
something of infinite worth. I'm willing to risk it
all for you.

SAY YES TO GOD

○ Spend some time reflecting on the ways God has
changed your mind, heart, and attitudes as you have read
Say Yes to God. If you have a reading partner, share some
of these reflections the next time you get together.

○ Pray right now for your brothers and sisters in God's
family who are being persecuted for their commitment
to Jesus Christ.

○ Listen to Rick and Kay Warren's message "The Global
PEACE Plan" and Kay's message "Your Next Steps" at
www.kaywarren.com.

THE ADVENTURE CONTINUES

Since the publication of *Dangerous Surrender*, the earliest version of this book, I have had the amazing privilege of sharing the truths with thousands of people around the world. Many people have emailed, written, or called to tell me about their experiences of saying yes to God and the incredible journey or adventure that ensued. Every one of these stories is told by an ordinary man or woman. Some are young, some old, some right in the middle of life — but each has one common denominator: he or she was willing to believe a *loving God* was asking for their deepest surrender, and as a result, they jumped into an unknown future, trusting him to catch them. What they found was what I have found: purpose, meaning, significance, joy in pain, increased intimacy with God, and the thrill of partnering with God in *his* world. I share these stories with you to encourage you in your own journey of saying yes to God.

○

"I finished the book in two days because I could not put it down, and at one point, I sat sobbing when reading a particular chapter. Your words went straight to my heart. I believe I am being called to work closely with my pastor and church in the HIV/AIDS ministry. Your book may have just pushed me over the edge to get very much involved." — Kate

"My husband and I operate a children's home in Sierra Leone, West Africa. We have used your book as a textbook read for those who have traveled with us in the past, and we've found it to be life changing for those who are new to saying yes to God when it comes to caring for orphans. We have adopted a child from Sierra Leone and have recently felt God calling us to adopt again — perhaps a child who is HIV positive. We know God can make a way." — Erica

○

"I just read your book, and it had me crying loudly. I am seeing everything differently and am feeling scared, but I will read it again. I have a heart to provide both shelter and retraining to women and children trapped in the sex industry in the red-light district of Bangkok." — Linda

○

"My husband purchased your book for me as a Christmas gift. It was perfect because it really helped me realize that those desires for helping children and for teaching others about worship, true corporate worship, are what God placed in my heart. At this point, I am a young mother, and serving outside of the home more than inside the home is not an option — but I know I can be involved in small ways. I will wait and just serve to the best of my ability." — Tiffany

○

"I am writing to let you know that God is using you to totally change my outlook on serving Christ. Please pray that I may have the courage to make the surrender that the Lord is asking of me. I have had my eyes opened by this book. I'm in the process of realizing that God wants me, first and foremost, to enter into intimate fellowship with him and to allow the leading and serving to be his and not my own. I look forward to more growth in the Lord as I simply surrender to his presence and will." — Charles

○

"I have just finished reading your book, a book I bought a week ago on a business trip thousands of miles away from home in Singapore. I have been encouraged, challenged, and spurred on to recklessly abandon myself to Jesus." — Hugo

○

"I am reading your book, and it has made a huge impact on my life. We pastor a church in New Mexico and have been here for twenty years. Your transparency gave me the courage to search my own heart, and I experienced an overwhelming presence of my heavenly Father. I respect you so much for your honesty that you openly share in the book." — Kathy

○

"I was desperate for some answers and horrified that my life was so busy I didn't have room to care about millions of people who are suffering and dying. Reading your book has been like reading my story. God has shown me that he is the solution to the suffering in the world, and I've grown to be passionate about our role as Christians in sharing his love and compassion. I thank God every day for rescuing me from myself." — BJ

○

"I am almost finished with your book and can hardly put it down long enough to write you this email. I have wept through most of it and am so touched, inspired, and impressed that I, too, am praying for God to open doors and give the wisdom and guidance to know when to walk through. I am seventy-seven and lost my darling husband of sixty years just recently. I definitely know it was no accident that I found your book." — Betty

○

"I was in Ethiopia with my second HIV-positive adopted child, not knowing if she would survive to return to the U.S. with me. Well, oddly enough, your book was on the shelf at the guesthouse I was staying at. I can't tell you how the Lord used that book to define what my husband and I had already done — things we really couldn't explain. People thought we were *crazy* to adopt a child in the last stages of AIDS. But it's because we're gloriously ruined and dangerously surrendered! Your book was such a comfort to me during a very difficult time. What a joy and relief to surrender!" — Carolyn

○

"I have to tell you that the message I heard you deliver at the Cry of the Orphan Summit in Fort Lauderdale was the most powerful message I believe I have ever heard. You were pointing your finger at yourself and not at the audience, and that is why it was so easy to receive (and yet so difficult). Carol and I have decided to adopt, not one, but two, international orphans as a result of what we hear the Lord saying to us since our time at Summit IV. The fruit of your vulnerability and surrender to the Lord continues to ripple out far and wide. Thank you for giving your "YES" to our heavenly Father." — Glenn

○

"As I finished your book last night, I prayed for God to show me what he wants me to do with this newly pledged surrender. I really, really meant it. I honestly don't think I've ever read anything so personally challenging — ever. Challenging because God used it to ask me for complete surrender at a level I have never experienced before." — Lori

○

"I became dangerously surrendered and stepped out of the comfortable to pursue the calling that the Lord had placed on my heart. Even though many people warned me not to go, I still pursued and surrendered, and I am forever ruined. I have now taken on a role with a national prison ministry to be an area coordinator to help assimilate prisoners back into the community and church, as well as reaching out to those still serving time and in prison for life. I have never seen such freedom within these walls. The church could learn something from these broken women." — Cris

○

"I have now become a dangerous believer! Your book should come with a warning label: Don't read this book unless you are ready for what God has in mind! After I read your book, God prompted me to become cofounder of a ministry called Oasis House. We are a women's center that reaches out to women who work in strip clubs. We take home-cooked meals into the clubs and serve women. We build relationships and ask, "How can we pray for you?" We used to be called the church ladies; now a lot of women call us Mom." — Donna

○

"I have been reading your book, and honestly, I have to read a little bit at a time because it does RUIN me every time. My heart just breaks in half! My husband and I know God is asking us to surrender everything we have and simply serve. Our hearts are willing. I keep saying to God, 'Just send me, I will go.'" — Lindsey

These are just a tiny sampling of the responses I receive on a weekly basis. These folks summoned up their last bits of courage and said yes to God. What about you? Will you join the Ranks of the Resistance — those disturbed, surrendered, ruined disciples of Jesus Christ who have determined to follow him to the end, no matter where it leads? Let today be the day you say yes to God!

www.KayWarren.com

At KayWarren.com you will find information to help you take the next step to **say yes to God**. Find featured resources that will enhance your reading experience in the chapter reviews and small group curriculum. Download the audio version of the book. Sign up for the 30-day adventure — and get ready for an adventure you won't want to miss.

Visit www.KayWarren.com, email Kay@KayWarren.com, or call the office of Kay Warren at (949) 609-8552.

Free iPhone App

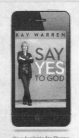

Download the free iPhone app titled "Kay Warren" where you will find video messages from Kay, helpful resources, and daily challenges to courageously surrender every part of your life to God. This app will encourage and empower you to continually **say yes to God**.

Visit www.KayWarren.com, email Kay@KayWarren .com, or call the office of Kay Warren at (949) 609-8552.

The HIV/AIDS Initiative

The devastating HIV/AIDS pandemic is providing the church the greatest opportunity to serve the hurting like Jesus did, to show God's love to skeptics, to share the Good News of God's tender love and mercy, and to extend a helping hand in communities around the world.

Visit www.hivandthechurch.com, email hiv@saddleback.com, or call (949) 609-8555.

The Orphan Care Connection

There are 143 million orphans and vulnerable children who need assistance — education, health care, and, most of all, a home. While not everyone is called to adopt, every Christian can find meaningful ways to care for these little ones through churches at home and around the world.

Visit www.orphansandthechurch.com, email orphans@saddleback.com, or call (949) 609-8555.

ACKNOWLEDGMENTS

My husband, Rick, is an amazing man. I knew when we met as goofy seventeen-year-olds that there was something unique about him. I had never known anyone quite like him, and I still don't. He is in a class by himself. I like routine; he loves change — eats it up, in fact! But the one thing that has never changed about him is his passionate love for me. He has always been my biggest cheerleader and fan, pushing me to develop and use my gifts, often over my protests of "I can't do that!" He saw potential in me long before I saw it in myself. He believes in me and enthusiastically shares messages, platforms, and the spotlight with me. I can't imagine ever doing life without him — my husband, pastor, and best friend of thirty-five years.

Our children, Amy, Joshua, and Matthew — plus their spouses, Tommy and Jaime — fill my life with delight. Watching them go through the stages and become young adults and form their own families is marvelous. And the grandkids? Oh my, they are the *best*! Kaylie, Cassidy, Caleb, and Cole have Grammy and Papa firmly wrapped around their tiny little fingers — we're crazy about them! My family is what keeps me grounded — they are the stable, constant source of love, encouragement, pleasure, and joy in my life. Thanks, kids, for being so patient while I was writing —

encouraging me, praying for me, reading the early manuscript and giving your honest feedback. I love you so much.

My mom and dad deserve many thanks. It was their constant encouragement to write that started the dream decades ago and their gentle nudges that kept it alive. My only sadness is that my daddy went home to be with the Lord in 2006. We didn't get to celebrate the fulfillment of the dream together here on earth, but I'm sure I heard whoops of excitement in heaven the day I completed the manuscript. Thanks, Dad — you taught me to love Jesus and inspired me to write. Thanks, Mom — your pleasure and pride in me are reward enough.

God knew that the journey he was sending me on would be a tough one and that I would need a close friend to share it with. He sent me a sacred companion in Elizabeth Styffe. Thanks, Elizabeth, for allowing God to seriously disturb you about suffering and for teaching me about living as a gloriously ruined woman. We've been around the world together — from presidential palaces to mud huts — and your presence has made the wonderful more wonderful and the unbearable more bearable. Partnership in ministry is the richest kind of fellowship on this earth, and I'm forever grateful for you.

My small group of three other couples (there were four couples, but Bucky and Joann moved back to Tennessee!) is my lifeline. We've committed to do life together. Births, deaths, weddings, funerals, cancer, surgeries, job crises, family emergencies, financial stress — we've been through it all and plan to grow old together. You guys cheer me on when I need encouragement, gently correct me when I'm off base, pray for me when I'm ready to chuck it all, bring me ice cream when I'm at my lowest, point me to Jesus as the only solution to my deepest struggles, and have promised to help me become the godly woman I long to be. Thanks, Tom and Chaundel, Brett and Dee, Glenn and Elizabeth — and my honey, Rick.

When I became interested in HIV/AIDS, I knew absolutely nothing. I had a very steep learning curve ahead of me! God provided numerous teachers, mentors, and friends along the way: Steve Haas, Debbie Dortzbach, Dr. Robert Redfield, Dr. Robb Sheneberger, Dr. Athanase Kiromera, Dr. Carla Alexander, Dr. Paul Cimoch, Dr. Rebecca Kuhn, and Shepherd and Anita Smith.

Many thanks to the wonderful folks at Zondervan and to my editor and friend, Cindy Lambert. Thanks as well to Sandra Vander Zicht and Dirk Buursma.

BIBLE TRANSLATIONS

NOTES

1. Gary Thomas, *Seeking the Face of God* (Eugene, Ore.: Harvest House, 1994), 95.
2. François Fénelon, *The Seeking Heart* (Beaumont, Tex.: SeedSowers, 1992), 125.
3. Quoted in Maria Coffey, *Explorers of the Infinite* (New York: Penguin, 2008), 99.
4. Thomas, *Seeking the Face of God*, 91.
5. Fénelon, *Seeking Heart*, 79.
6. Fénelon, *Seeking Heart*, 99.
7. C. S. Lewis, *The Lion, the Witch and the Wardrobe* (1950; repr., New York: HarperCollins, 1994), 80.
8. Fénelon, *Seeking Heart*, 3 – 4.
9. Fénelon, *Seeking Heart*, 25.
10. Jake Thoene, *Shaiton's Fire* (Wheaton, Ill.: Tyndale House, 2001), 240.
11. Martin Luther King Jr., *Stride Toward Freedom* (1958; repr., Boston: Beacon, 2010), 39.
12. Henri J. M. Nouwen, *Out of Solitude* (Notre Dame, Ind.: Ave Maria, 1974), 42 – 43.
13. Nouwen, *Out of Solitude*, 43.
14. Nouwen, *Out of Solitude*, 40 – 41.
15. Lewis Smedes, *How Can It Be All Right When Everything Is All Wrong?* (rev. ed.; San Francisco: HarperSanFrancisco, 1992), 75.
16. Cited in Mother Teresa, *A Simple Path* (New York: Ballantine, 1995), 88.
17. Fénelon, *Seeking Heart*, 17.
18. Oswald Chambers, *My Utmost for His Highest* (New York: Dodd, Mead & Co., 1935), 6 (January 6).
19. Henri J. M. Nouwen, *Can You Drink the Cup?* (Notre Dame, Ind.: Ave Maria, 1996), 57.

20. Dietrich Bonhoeffer, *Life Together* (San Francisco: HarperSanFrancisco, 1954), 94.

21. Dietrich Bonhoeffer, *Letters and Papers from Prison*, ed. Eberhard Bethge (New York: Macmillan, 1971), 382.

22. Dietrich Bonhoeffer, *The Cost of Discipleship* (New York: Macmillan, 1959), 99.

23. Chambers, *My Utmost for His Highest*, 274 (September 30).

24. John Baillie, *A Diary of Private Prayer* (New York: Scribner, 1949), 113.

READERS' GROUP DISCUSSION GUIDE

by Cindy Lambert

CHAPTER 1
THE LEAP OF FAITH

1. Have you ever experienced God persistently working to direct your attention to some relationship, issue, or cause? If so, describe a major turning point in your realization.

2. Kay describes the frustration of thinking that the AIDS pandemic was such a gigantic problem that she, as an ordinary person, wasn't equipped to make a difference. Consider two or three world problems that deeply trouble you. Do you believe you can have any significant impact on these problems? Why or why not?

3. When was the last time you initiated conversation on a "disturbing" topic? Why do people avoid such conversations? Discuss how such conversations can be destructive or constructive.

4. Read Kay's discussion of the world's wealthy. By her standards, are you wealthy? If so, do you concur with her assessment of "legitimate guilt"? Discuss why or why not.

5. Consider this chapter's examples of Mary and the McClendons as lives courageously surrendered to God. Name a biblical character or contemporary example that impresses you as a life courageously surrendered. How do these stories speak to you? Identify the factors that draw you to these examples.

CHAPTER 2
THE KINGDOM OF ME

1. Make a list of the key reasons you don't want to get too involved with people in dire need. Reflect on Kay's question, "Who or what can change your perspective in such a way that instead of living to serve yourself, you actually *want* to live to serve someone else?" How would you answer this question?

2. What does Kay identify as the command lying at the heart of courageous surrender? In what way is this the beginning step in learning to be a disciple?

3. Kay writes, "This is how we grow into spiritual maturity." How would you summarize her reasoning in your own words?

4. Kay explains that her growing understanding of God's sovereign design created an expectation that God would someday use her for his good purposes. Describe your current sense of the purposes God may have in store for you.

5. Kay describes the WITTY principle and then concludes, "Figuring out [God's] ways isn't any of my business. Following him is." Which of God's ways have been most challenging for you to accept and follow?

CHAPTER 3
GLORIOUSLY RUINED

1. Kay describes being "gloriously ruined." In your own words how would you define her meaning of this phrase? Do you find the prospect of being gloriously ruined repulsive, frightening, attractive, or desirable? Why?

2. This chapter describes the concept of simultaneously living in "three worlds." Describe the "worlds" of your own life experience thus far. Are you open to having God introduce a new world into your life? Reflect on what that could look like for you.

3. Kay asks, "In what ways are you allowing [God] to rearrange your schedule, your finances, your affections, so you can regularly interact with those he loves?" How would you answer this question?

4. The final paragraph of the chapter describes the paradox of becoming seriously disturbed and gloriously ruined as the best thing Kay has ever experienced. Given the "cost" she has described, what do you understand as her reason for feeling that the benefits far outweigh the cost? Name some of your own challenging circumstances where the rewards outweigh the very high cost.

CHAPTER 4

READY, SET, STOP

1. Consider a detour in your own life — a time when you suddenly found yourself facing an unwelcome change in direction. At the time, how did it affect your understanding of and relationship to God?

2. Kay identifies two choices in the face of crisis: pull away from or turn toward God. Apply these two options to the scenario in question 1 above. Imagine the actions and results involved in pulling away from God. Imagine the actions and results involved in running toward him. Discuss what you discover during this exercise.

3. "What is God's explanation for this broken system?" Kay cried out to her friend Elizabeth. Yet she concludes in this chapter that God is absolutely worthy of our trust. In your own words, explain how Kay bridges the gap between these two seemingly opposite perspectives. What is the condition of your own "bridge" between the reality of suffering and the trustworthiness of God?

4. Contemplate your willingness to lash yourself to the mast, as Kay describes it. What cost would you pay for doing so? What is the cost if you do not do so?

5. Read Job 23:8 – 10, then reread verse 9 aloud. Note the phrase "when he is at work." Picture your greatest suffering or fears as north, east, south, and west, then read the paragraph surrounding Kay's motto, "Control the controllables and leave the uncontrollables to God." What would you need to surrender to join Kay in her refrain?

6. Kay describes an epiphany in the bamboo hut with the suffering Cambodian woman. How did this epiphany transform her ministry?

CHAPTER 5

EXPOSING EVIL

1. *Click.* Do you identify with Kay's desire to change the channel to avoid exposure to the evil in our world? With what emotions and thoughts did you struggle as you read this chapter?

2. Kay writes, "What could I do against such despicable evil? I was just an ordinary woman." Yet she did choose to personally engage in the battle. What moved her from her state of helplessness to her proactive response of becoming involved?

3. Review the list of those engaged in pushing back the darkness. Consider the lives and deeds of people you know who are playing an active part in bringing light into dark places. Name two you admire and discuss the impact they have had.

4. What weapons has God provided for our battle against evil? Choose one in which you find the most encouragement, and explain why.

5. Kay describes what God does not want us to do in the face of evil. Identify the undesirable response into which you are most prone to slip. What could strengthen your resolve to avoid that response?

6. How has this chapter made you uncomfortable or challenged your thinking? Select one uncomfortable thought from this chapter that you will use to engage in a meaningful conversation this week.

CHAPTER 6

MIRRORS DON'T LIE

1. What does Kay mean by the phrase "the mirror doesn't lie"? Were you taken aback by the shift from righteous indignation to the dramatic statement "The harsh reality is that given the right circumstance, any one of us is capable of any deed"?

2. Read the quote from Henri Nouwen that follows the phrase. Do you find yourself agreeing with or resisting his premise?

3. Consider Kay's metaphor of Carlsbad Caverns. Take a few minutes to privately consider the very worst of yourself buried deep within your own subterranean caves. Are you afraid that God is shocked and repulsed by what he finds there? Are you prepared to invite God to flood your deepest crevices?

4. Kay identifies a truth that "changes everything." In what way does this truth change you?

5. How would you summarize this chapter's connection between understanding our own depravity and our personal involvement in ministering to the needs of others?

6. As you review this challenging chapter, look for all the good news, naming every positive truth you find encouraging. How does this final exercise affect your response to this chapter?

CHAPTER 7

THE GIFT OF PRESENCE

1. In this chapter Kay describes a transformation in her understanding of the essence of compassionate service. Contrast her understanding at the beginning of the chapter with her understanding at the end.

2. Discuss the various levels of impact we can have on those in need:

   • providing physical labor

   • speaking words of truth

   • simply being compassionately present

   Do you tend to place a higher value on one over the others? Why or why not?

3. How might the thought of being a *container of God* influence your impression of what you have to offer to a hurting world?

4. Why did many of the residents of the leprosarium in the Philippines who were already cured of leprosy remain there? Compare their experiences with that of people who bear the "scars" of broken lives as they consider visiting or joining a church.

5. Name specific improvements a local congregation can implement to become a place of greater welcome and safety for those who bear the scars of brokenness.

6. Kay writes, "To make a difference, you don't have to have a grand strategy for eliminating poverty, HIV/AIDS, illiteracy, greed, or suffering." What *is* needed? How does this realization affect your willingness to personally engage with a hurting world?

CHAPTER 8

A DELIBERATE CHOICE

1. Reread the quote from Lewis Smedes. Has anyone ever willingly entered into your life's pain in the way Smedes describes? Have you ever felt God's pull to do so in the life of another? Describe what happens in the heart of a sufferer who is on the receiving end of such mercy.

2. Take a few private moments to be completely vulnerable before God. What about this chapter seems most threatening to you or your current lifestyle?

3. Consider these words: *shocked, angry, frustrated, guilty, troubled, wrestling, resistant, stirred, hopeful, inspired, called, compelled.* Choose the three words that come closest to describing what you are experiencing as you are reading this book. Explain your choices.

4. How has your understanding of HIV/AIDS, world poverty, social justice, and the experiences of the outcast been affected by Kay's experiences and perspective?

5. Reread each surrender question at the end of chapters 1 through 8. Identify which have been the easiest and which have caused the most wrestling.

6. Discuss specific opportunities you've become aware of in which you could invest yourself in compassionate service.

CHAPTER 9
AN UNEXPECTED BOND

1. In what ways do you identify with Kay's perceptions of prostitutes at the opening of this chapter? How would you compare them to your own perceptions of people who are HIV positive?

2. Kay writes, "There were profound spiritual truths hidden in that encounter with these outcast women." Discuss the truths you find in this encounter and identify the most unexpected insight you gain.

3. Reread the story of Kay's encounter with Pastor Mike. Choose one sentence you would most like to discuss and turn it into a question for your group to discuss.

4. Read the following verses recounting the emotions that Jesus felt: Matthew 21:12; 23:37; Luke 13:15 – 16; 17:2; John 11:35. Compare those emotions to what you have felt as you have read this book so far.

5. How would you describe Kay's discovery that transformed her despair and hopelessness into an unexpected bond with Jesus?

6. The title of this chapter is "An Unexpected Bond." Select one unexpected insight that you have found particularly meaningful.

CHAPTER 10
LINKING ARMS

1. In what ways can you identify with Kay's sense of despair as she witnessed her first International AIDS Conference in Bangkok? What infiltration of evil in your world do you find overwhelming?

2. Reread Acts 26:12 – 23, then focus on verses 17 and 18. As you anticipate your next twelve months, is it conceivable that you are also being "sent off"? If you were to choose an area of service, what might it be? Does this question fill you with anxiety or anticipation?

3. "The only problem is that it's impossible." Kay jolts the reader with these words. List several biblical examples of God's accomplishing the seemingly impossible. Recount the names of God's servants chosen and empowered to play critical roles in those events.

4. In the midst of her discussion of the history of the Christian church, Kay asks the question, "So why would I put any faith at all in such a ragtag bunch of losers? Because God does." What is your understanding of why God works through people rather than solely through divine, supernatural means?

5. Discuss the range of roles the church has played in world history — from heroic to horrific. If you were to interview local residents about the impact of your church on your community or the world, how might they respond?

6. "We don't go after global Goliaths armed only with our personal slingshots," writes Kay. Reread her description of how the body works together. How can your local church — how can you — link arms to join the movement to become God's hands and feet for a broken world?

CHAPTER 11
WHAT ARE YOU WILLING TO DIE FOR?

1. Can you imagine your own Polaroid picture of God's will for you developing over the years? What do you know now about God's purposes for you that you did not yet "see" two years ago? Is there an area of your life where the fuzziness is giving way to a sharper image?

2. How is it possible that the center of God's will can be the safest yet most dangerous place to be?

3. Kay writes, "Most of us are called to pay a much smaller price, although each point of surrender can at times turn into high drama as we play tug-of-war with God." What are the "high drama" points in your tug-of-war with God thus far in your life? What part have they played in your developing maturity?

4. What great surrender challenges do you see ahead? Do you find yourself dreading them or eagerly awaiting them? How can such challenges craft you into Christlikeness?

5. Of all the stirring images in this chapter, which had the most profound effect on you? Why?

ABOUT
KAY WARREN

KAY WARREN IS USING HER FAR-REACHING INFLUENCE AS A voice for the weak and vulnerable.

In 2002, Warren became, in her words, "seriously disturbed" by the suffering of the millions infected with or affected by HIV/AIDS. Through the PEACE plan, she is now challenging the worldwide church to take on not just AIDS but the global giants of spiritual darkness, poverty, disease, ignorance, and lack of servant leaders as well.

Warren frequently travels around the globe to encourage HIV-positive men, women, and vulnerable children, and today she is a powerful advocate on their behalf. In 2004, she began the HIV/AIDS Initiative at Saddleback Church and serves as its founder.

In 2005, she was instrumental in presenting Saddleback Church's first HIV/AIDS conference. The Global Summit on AIDS and the Church was held in 2005, 2006, and 2007. Warren launched the HIV/AIDS Caring Community in 2006. Located at www.hivandthechurch.com, the online community offers resources and inspiration for individuals and churches involved in HIV/AIDS ministry. Her passion for caring for orphans and vulnerable children is reflected in the website www.orphansandthechurch.com. Many of her messages and videos, as well as featured resources for Say Yes to God, can be found at www.kaywarren.com.

As a two-time cancer survivor, Warren knows firsthand how a life-threatening diagnosis alters one's daily life. Her own bouts with suffering have motivated her to serve others who are sick. She has come face-to-face with the hurting as a volunteer in her own community; at Mother Teresa's Home for the Dying in Calcutta, India; at the leper colony and AIDS hospice in Manila, Philippines; and with World Vision, World Relief, and The International Justice Mission in Thailand and Cambodia. In Mozambique, Malawi, South Africa, Kenya, Uganda, and Rwanda she has ministered to those living with HIV/AIDS through several organizations, as well as through Saddleback Church's partnership with local African churches. She has become a student of HIV/AIDS and attended the XV International AIDS Conference in Bangkok, Thailand; the XVI International AIDS Conference in Toronto, Canada; the XVII International AIDS Conference in Mexico City, Mexico; and the XVIII International AIDS Conference in Vienna, Austria.

As a speaker, Warren has been a voice for suffering individuals. In addition to being featured at various Purpose Driven Church and Radicalis conferences, Warren has addressed many government, church, academic, and professional groups, including the Government Women Leaders of Rwanda, the Management Association of the Philippines, the Learning Community of Willow Creek Church, the Nootbaar Institute at Pepperdine University School of Law, Loma Linda University School of Public Health, and numerous other colleges and universities. She cohosted with her husband, Rick, the Saddleback Civil Forum on Global Health, honoring President and Mrs. George Bush. Recognized for her passion and influence, Warren has spoken at The Global Coalition on Women and AIDS (UNAIDS) and at the Ecumenical Pre-Conference of both the XVI International AIDS Conference in Toronto and the XVII International AIDS Conference in Mexico City.

In 2006, Warren was among eight women honored at the CNN Inspire Summit, which recognized women for their impact on global issues through political, social, and humanitarian efforts that have inspired others to get involved. In 2008, she was awarded the Distinguished Service Award from Loma Linda University's School of Public Health.

An accomplished writer, Warren's doctrinal study, *Foundations*, coauthored with Tom Holladay, won a Gold Medallion Award in 2004. Her book, *Dangerous Surrender*, was released in December 2007, and the revised and expanded softcover edition, retitled *Say Yes to God*, is now available. She has contributed to *The aWAKE Project: Uniting Against the African AIDS Crisis*. Additionally, she has been a columnist for *Christianity Today* and *Purpose Driven Connection* magazines. Kay has written for CNN.com and the *Washington Post*. She has been featured in *POZ, Reader's Digest, Guideposts, Today's Christian Woman, Missions Mosaic, Sojourners, Seed, Worship, Worship Leader, Encouraging Women, Good*, and *OC Metro* magazines.

In 1980, Warren and her husband began Saddleback Church in the living room of their condominium. Now one of the largest churches in America, Saddleback Church has given Warren a platform for influencing Christians and other leaders worldwide.

Raised in the rich heritage of a Christian home, Warren attended California Baptist College and earned her BA from California State University, Los Angeles. She is mother to Amy, Joshua, and Matthew, and grandmother to Kaylie, Cassidy, Caleb, and Cole. She and her husband reside in Southern California.

Share Your Thoughts

With the Author: Your comments will be forwarded to
the author when you send them to *zauthor@zondervan.com*.

With Zondervan: Submit your review of this book
by writing to *zreview@zondervan.com*.

Free Online Resources at

www.zondervan.com

Zondervan AuthorTracker: Be notified whenever your favorite
authors publish new books, go on tour, or post an update
about what's happening in their lives at www.zondervan.com/
authortracker.

Daily Bible Verses and Devotions: Enrich your life with daily
Bible verses or devotions that help you start every morning
focused on God. Visit www.zondervan.com/newsletters.

Free Email Publications: Sign up for newsletters on Christian
living, academic resources, church ministry, fiction, children's
resources, and more. Visit www.zondervan.com/newsletters.

Zondervan Bible Search: Find and compare Bible passages in
a variety of translations at www.zondervanbiblesearch.com.

Other Benefits: Register yourself to receive online benefits
like coupons and special offers, or to participate in research.

ZONDERVAN®

ZONDERVAN.com/
AUTHORTRACKER
follow your favorite authors